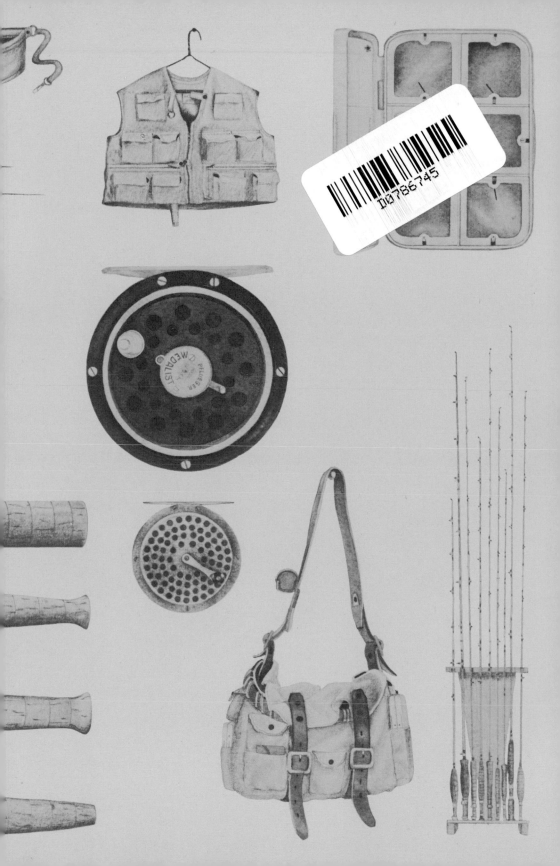

FLY
TACKLE

Also by Harmon Henkin
THE ENVIRONMENT, THE ESTABLISHMENT AND THE LAW

FLY
TACKLE

A Guide to the Tools of the Trade

Harmon Henkin

Illustrations by Jeff Johnson

J. B. LIPPINCOTT COMPANY
Philadelphia and New York

U.S. LIBRARY OF CONGRESS CATALOGING IN PUBLICATION DATA

Henkin, Harmon.
    Fly tackle: a guide to the tools of the trade.

    Bibliography: p.
    Includes index.
    1. Fishing tackle. 2. Fly fishing. I. Title.
SH447.H46   799.1′2   75–18644
ISBN–0–397–01072–9

To Richard, Laura and the Harrimans,
in the hope that Joshua will have places to use fly tackle.

Contents

Some Reflections on Tackle

I

Angling writer Edward Hewitt once noted in his inimitable style that trout anglers ideally pass through three stages. In the first period they try to catch as many fish as possible. The next stage finds the journeyman trying to land as large a fish as possible. In the third stage, true angling maturity is achieved and the goal is catching fish under the most difficult conditions possible.

Well, tackle buffs go through similar stages. In the first, while in Michigan at college, I tried to gather up (if not actually monopolize) the Western world's production of tackle for the last century, with little regard to merit. During the second stage, I went for only the cream of the tackle world—not stopping with rods, for instance, till I had a Payne, Garrison, Leonard and a couple of other luminaries. That their actions were either too soft or too tippy bothered me only occasionally—when I fished, for example! The second stage went by the board when I realized that I had fished most of 1969 with a $50 Scientific Angler System 6 rather than those angling artifacts holding up my den wall.

Now, with at least one foot in the third stage, I own five rods which allow me to fish passably anywhere in the world (though perhaps not on Venus, where the high gravity probably requires a very powerful rod). When I get tired of a rod I swap it off for another that seems, at least for the moment, better suited for whatever angling scheme is possessing me at the time. No rod really seems the ultimate weapon any longer. A tackle Don Juan, I can appreciate most rods without a lifetime commitment or promises of undying love. I fish them hard and then bid them adieu without a tear—usually.

This mellowing process took place when I came to realize that fly-fishing, cleared of the muddle that envelops it, has a simple, primary aim—to catch fish. That is the only real, valid reason for throwing a fly upon the water. Almost from the beginnings of the sport, however, there have been some grand experts and authors who hold as their theme that somehow fly-fishing isn't about catching fish. Their supposition is that it is an admixture of aesthetics, philosophy and science, and that by standing in cold water for a couple of hours you can communicate with your God (obviously not a bait fisherman). Certainly all these elements are present in the recreation, but they are important elements of all the better parts of life, not just fly-fishing.

In its highest reaches, the sport is a holistic way of coming to grips with the natural environment. When fly-fishing you can be as integrated into your surroundings as is possible for the alienated species that is man, living in a dehumanized society. But like all biological entities, we are goal-oriented, and in fly-fishing the goal is tricking fish. To deny this is to reject the essence of this or any other sport and to reduce it to something essentially meaningless. Of course, we have all known the athletic angler for whom the rivers are places to demonstrate distance casting, and I have known quite a few businessmen for whom spring creeks were floating golf courses where business deals were consummated. I have also known hairy mountain freaks for whom trout streams were created as environments for dropping acid or mescaline. But these diversions have little to do with true angling.

What these weighty thoughts mean to someone freezing their butt off in a river is simple. To give priority to the accumulation of as many rods or even as many great rods as possible is really antithetical to the organic process that fishing should be. It is something else. This accumulation becomes another exercise in consumerism—albeit an advanced one—more things to fill up lives already cluttered with things rather than genuine experiences. It is sad to progress beyond the level of responding to TV soap commercials only to respond to the unspoken cultural commercials that inform us that we can have the same sort of angling fulfillment that deodorants give to our social lives if only we get that particularly snazzy, custom-built 7½-footer.

This is one of the big lies of twentieth-century America.

There is an unbridgeable gap between the pride that a craftsman has in fine tools which are used to do fine things and the mock pride in rote ownership of something that is fine in sterile isolation. Though fine tackle contains a sense of history and artisanship lacking in the glittering wares of the discount house, fishing equipment was created for utilitarian reasons. The function of fishing is to catch fish; the function of tackle is to be a tool in that process.

Sensitive, responsive tackle can definitely increase fly-fishing pleasure, but only if you are honestly aware of the difference between quality and mundane equipment. But this same fine, sensitive tackle will ultimately lead to dissatisfaction if the stuff is hung on the wall and peered at like a Tasmanian stamp collection or stuffed aardvark. Tackle is not meant to be an end unto itself, though it is an easy cultural fallacy to believe otherwise. Even the willowy, weak-butted rods of a hundred years ago were meant to cast flies and function as best the technology and theory of the day would allow, and to look at them as mere historic objets d'art is to give them a one-dimensionality never intended. The great rodmaker Ev Garrison once told me, "My rods were made to be fished, not stared at." Yet it is tempting to merely look at and fondle the elegant, classic simplicity of a Garrison or Payne without using it. Such esteemed, valuable possessions are part of the glamour syndrome; we have relationships with people and things because they look great and have status, regardless of what's inside them. Then with time's passage we become disillusioned because they don't, of themselves, magically bring us happiness, and we begin again the search for the Holy Grail.

We are a nation of collectors, filling the empty spaces in our lives with everything from cigarette lighters and empty whiskey bottles to antique cars and fly rods—neglecting their intrinsic function. Different classes of people collect different things. The very wealthy have their art and racehorses, the middle echelons their books and stamps and the bottom levels their knick-knacks and matchbooks. But it is all really the same, a way of giving us a sense of value, a sense of place, a sense of what is lacking in our lives.

When a trout or tarpon is being stalked, tackle assumes its rightful function as a mere physical extension of our psyche. As long as it does this task without unduly bothering us, so that we can concentrate on the fish, it is fine tackle. Only a severely jaded person or a tackle rep would think of equipment at such a time. Tackle is incidental to the basic encounter between two creatures.

It makes no difference at those crucial moments whether the rod eagerly clutched is a Thomas or Peak or Fenwick, and it is those rare moments that are the essence of sport. All of the preparatory time is merely preparatory time. Those moments are authentic in lives marked overwhelmingly by inauthenticity.

Fishing wouldn't have much purpose if it couldn't help us live a little more genuinely. But, thank goodness, it can and does.

II

There are many reasons why tackle, the most visible symbol of fly-fishing, has such a lure for anglers.

Equipment is obviously of great historical importance to the sport, and changes in it are the result of major theoretical developments and the work of great technical innovators, recorded by towering literary figures. Fine tackle is also an example of fine workmanship, a quality that transcends the limitations of any sport. For the real connoisseur, individual rods illustrate the unique techniques of the master builders. A reel like the Hardy Perfect, with its ball bearings, is a working illustration of a simple but exact mechanical principle. Although fishing equipment may seem fairly simple compared to that of many other sports, angling is, as they used to say of baseball, a game of mere inches, and subtle differences in rod design, line taper and leader diameter magnify terrifically while fishing. So there are plenty of legitimate reasons for the angler to take more than a passing interest in the tools of his trade.

But there is also a historical reason why tackle mania is so rampant and dominates fly-fishing more than equipment fetishism influences other sports.

As John McDonald and other angling scholars have noted, the growth of sport fishing roughly parallels the growth of the merchant class. Its popularity has risen with the growing strength of the bourgeoisie over the last five centuries, and this group has traditionally been concerned with the status that various commodities bring. Since the merchant class is not born with an inbred nobility, it achieves exalted status through the accumulation of property.

The first, and for a long period the only, major organized

Tackle on the porch

sports in Europe were the so-called blood field sports like hunting. They belonged lock, stock and hunting horn to the aristocracy. The growing middle class developed its own recreations, and it seems to me that the merchants' most important early contribution to the sporting tradition was angling. It became as perfectly suited to their recreational tastes as Protestantism became suited to their religious inclinations. Both fishing and Protestantism were basically individual endeavors, requiring little social lineage.

In the nineteenth century the working class finally began to make itself felt as an economic and political force. Workers were making menacing noises about their treatment by factory owners.

There were even a few revolutions, and the rich became uneasy about their privileged position. One of the defenses of a social group under attack is to further define its role by graphing society into those who behave "right" and those who don't, and this is the period when angling snobbery really hit, particularly in England.

For most of sport fishing's history there was little ethical difference between catching fish with artificials and naturals. Izaak Walton and most other revered early writers were either complete bait fishermen or fly-fished only when low-water conditions required it. In the late nineteenth century, however, when angling was being redefined so as to make sure only certain kinds of people would be its practitioners, innovators like Frederick Halford, the father of the dry fly, began to dogmatize about a once fairly loose activity. Soon the only thing for a proper English angler to do was to cast a dry fly to a rising fish.

In America, on the other hand, where we are all created semiequal, angling's class struggle has been fought less around tactics and more through what we know best, our commodities. Though some of the English dry-fly—and, more fundamentally, fly—snobbery hit our beaches, it has been our equipment that more clearly defines our social roles.

The fine bamboo rod, always an expensive item, has become a badge of honor, like a knight's sword. The better and more customized our rod, the better and more noble an angler we are presumed to be. The more money we can afford to spend on our tackle, the more esteem we accrue. The foolishness of our tackle mania thus came from our socioeconomic foibles. It has taken many of us years to accept this, and the residue is still deep enough to drown a horse.

You can see it on the porches of our fishing clubs, where tweedy fisherfolk congregate, martini glass in one hand, Leonard in the other. You can see it in many of the ads of our fancy rod-makers, Madison Avenue jargon slyly informing us that sooner or later we'll own Brand X rod and instantly be transformed into a real gentleman angler instead of an uncouth beer-swilling slob who fishes with a solid fiberglass rod and a closed-face spinning reel. It becomes ludicrous when the ads are translated into snobbery by anglers who might wet a line twice a year and who can barely cast, but for whom the ownership of a Winston or Orvis becomes a substitute for decent quality of life.

This tackle fetish is natural for Americans. To be brand-name conscious is part of our national heritage—like our love of fast cars or headache remedies. Meaningless differences in rods, magnified by a $100 difference in price, are taken to mean we are persons of unquestionable taste. It is sad, though not unusual, to see brand names become life names, and as we watch our waters destroyed by greed and indifference, we choose finer and finer tackle to fish less and less.

III

So, after all that, why on earth am I writing a book on fly tackle? A good question with a complicated answer.

There isn't any doubt that good, well-balanced equipment is a pleasure to use—even critical in some circumstances. Knowing your tools and how to use them enhances what fly-fishing is all about. The mechanical process of casting becomes second nature, integrated into the entire process of fishing, whereas tackle which is awkward to handle always intrudes disturbingly into your consciousness.

The act of respecting the delicacy, feel and workmanship of a great—or even a good—rod, suited for its function, is excellent for the fishing psyche. An appreciation of fine tackle can help while away the tedious hours, days or months between outings, giving your fishing a sense of continuity otherwise lacking. In learning to perceive subtle differences in rod taper and design, you will also learn about the differences in angling techniques that characterize various eras of the sport and that have landed us where we are. A thorough knowledge of your equipment also makes it easier to adapt to changing fishing situations, and you are less likely to fall into boring routines because of the limitations of your tackle.

It is getting very difficult for even the advanced angler to paw through the tons of glittering equipment available in stores and catalog shops and make the right choices for his kind of fishing. There is little in the way of a systematic approach to tackle, and prices have been climbing rapidly. If you have to shell out $100 or more and make a bad mistake because of some clerk's or writer's prejudices, the waste can sour you on the sport quickly.

This book will be an effort to correct this lack but also, and perhaps more importantly, it is a tribute to the beauty and quality of fine tackle, two attributes sadly lacking in most areas of modern life.

2

Materials for Rod Building

As of mid-1975, the three basic materials used in rod construction are bamboo—also referred to as cane—fiberglass and various sorts of graphites. Each has some advantages.

Bamboo will have more space devoted to it in this book than the others, mainly because there is much more to be understood about its history and crafting. Also, bamboo is potentially the most expensive, has more lore (and lure) and is the area where the beginning buyer gets raked over the coals most easily. Nobody is selling secondhand Fenwicks at high prices as collector's items, and no one is forging copies of Berkeleys.

Other than the values ascribed to it by those who swoon over the "feel" of bamboo, that mystical semireligious quality that true believers impart to wooden rods, there are a few concrete qualities that make bamboo a fine material for building rods. A Boeing engineer with whom I once shared a couple of days' angling in central Washington explained why he, a fastidious person, would use only bamboo. First, he said, was its shape. Bamboo rods are usually six-sided, and therefore their movements are controlled within the parameters of those sides.

In other words, with a glass rod, which is round, the tool accentuates casting errors by heading the motion in the direction of the error. If you cast a bit lopsided to the left, the rod will mirror that movement because there is nothing to attempt to keep it straight. With bamboo, on the other hand, the construction of sides tends to keep the motion going more in a straight back-and-forth pattern. Flick a glass rod and a bamboo rod side by side and you'll see what I mean. In essence, the bamboo affords an opportunity for more control.

Graphite blanks are also round and have a smaller diameter to boot, so they also tend to be less forgiving than bamboo in this regard. But, since they are stiffer and wobble less than glass, they are theoretically closer to bamboo than fiberglass is.

In the second place, bamboo is solid and fiberglass is hollow. This gives a cane rod more sensitivity and feel. If your rod is transmitting casts, fish or whatever through its whole diameter, it is going to tell more of the "story" than if the impulses are being carried only through a shell. Some of the early fiberglass rods were solid, but they were most often terrible contraptions. As a reformed sinner I will add, however, that they made wonderful spinning bait rods since they had a sensitivity lacking in the hollow glass rods that came to dominate the market. The solid rods were invariably floppy, wet-fly sorts and just too slow to cast comfortably.

Bamboo's solid feeling and resulting sensitivity are what most people mean when they talk of the uniqueness of cane. To me, the responsiveness of bamboo is most apparent in small rods, especially those used for dry flies. You do more false casting and precise presentation with rods under 8 feet, and the sensitivity of wood is a real plus for me.

On a custom level there are a few things that can be done with glass rods that help give them a solid feeling. Russ Peak, who makes the best glass rods yet created, will sometimes use plugs as dampeners to stiffen up his models. The Pasadena master craftsman did this on the four-piece, 8-foot parabolic-action rod he built for me. When I got it, the taper was just too slow for me to cast comfortably, as is usually the case with me and a full parabolic rod that bends all the way to the handle. I returned the rod, and Russ inserted a plug in the bottom section that stiffened up the action, making it more like the Paul Young Para 15 I normally use. This dampener also gave the rod a solid feel, actually the best feel on a glass rod I've ever handled. It is terrifically smooth despite its four sections. Of course, production rods don't undergo this tender loving care, or anything similar.

The graphites are of hollow construction and a bit too thin to transmit as well as bamboo. They are also very hard and dense, so the "feelings" jam together and are transmitted more quickly than with organic bamboo, where the impulses can be picked up

Cross section of fiberglass rod

individually. The transmission of energy goes through a greater area with bamboo than with graphite. Consequently, the casting impulse permeates the bamboo rod more gently than it does a graphite. This also makes bamboo more forgiving when errors are made.

The third reason for bamboo's eminence among rod materials is its ability to recover. Most glass rods shake, rattle and roll for a considerable time after a cast or flick, but bamboo will settle relatively quickly. This characteristic of glass rods was far worse in the past than it is today, now that manufacturers have become aware of the problem. The shaking has an adverse affect on your casting because the rod is vibrating the line, sending out minor ripples while the cast is in progress. Also a rod that recovers quickly can use all of its energy momentum to send the line in the required direction.

Beware of glass rods that take forever and a day to quiet down after motion is imparted to them. They are almost always of dismal quality.

Graphite, because of its high-density construction or stiffness, recovers very quickly. You flick it once and it goes up and back and then stops dead in its tracks, just like the best bamboo.

Those are the alleged reasons for the superiority of bamboo, but there are some pluses in the other camps as well. In larger rods there is no doubt that glass and graphite work much better for me. Graphite weighs roughly half as much as a comparable bamboo rod and about two thirds as much as a glass one. You have to be a bit dazed to cast a 6-ounce bamboo rod when a 4-ounce glass one will do the same job, especially if your fishing requires heaving out lots of line.

The first glass rods were greeted with all the hoopla that outdoor writers, magazines and manufacturers could muster. The few good ones in the early days were made by Conlon, by Silaflex and, to a lesser degree, by Shakespeare, probably the big innovator in the fiberglass field. Glass-rod technology came after the war as one of many carry-overs from the defense industries. It was quickly realized that fiberglass rods were practical, but their rapid acceptance by a noncritical fishing audience, the majority of whom were enamored of spin fishing, is probably the big reason why they improved so slowly. If the companies could sell their junk, why should they worry about making good products? Some of these early rods were incredibly terrible—unusable by today's standards.

Without getting very technical, hollow fiberglass rods are made by spinning glass fibers over a metal mandrel and catalyzing them with a resin. The taper of the mandrel is what decides the rod's action, and in the past these tapers have generally not been subtle enough. When the glass cools off, the mandrel is hydraulically removed and we have the blank. A rod blank, incidentally, is the term used to describe the one-piece stock as it comes from the factory without even ferrules added, except that in some retail stores blanks are sold with ferrules but nothing else. We are talking about factories with complex manufacturing processes, but this, in a nutshell, is how it's done. A great deal can be done with fiberglass design but, since they are almost all mass-produced, they are usually built to the concept of the lowest common denominator packaged to the highest possible degree. California custom builder Russ Peak has access to the manufacturing process of a large California blank producer, so he can customize his sticks. There are lots of questions about which "custom maker" gets which glass blanks from whom. This is quite a murky issue, too murky for a country boy like me to mess around in with any confidence.

As an aside, there are very few companies in the country making glass rod blanks. Most of the various brands come from a few big outfits, so their similarity is no accident. Individuality is not a general characteristic of glass rods, so be cautious in your shopping. Brand X at $5 may be the exact same blank that is being merchandised at $9.98 by another dealer. It is still possible to get a very usable blank for around $5 in 1975, though some of the more individualized ones by shops such as Winston get as much as $20. But Winston will give you almost any action or type blank for your money, whereas the cheaper blanks are normally in stock weights and actions. If you have specialized needs, you have to go to specialized concerns.

Graphite manufacturing is fairly similar to glass. It is actually a popularized term for a very stiff type of carbon fiber (no relationship to pencil carbon) that was synthesized by the English Royal Aircraft Establishment in 1965. The first recreational use of graphite—a term we'll use to describe all the new compounds—was in golf clubs. The Shakespeare Company discovered that the little round ball, which thank goodness keeps some potential anglers out of the water, could be hit further with a graphite shaft.

Some time after this, a smart fellow discovered that graphite could also help the poor but noble caster. The fibers were embedded in an epoxy resin and cured. The graphites have a much higher density than glass, and their design and tapers are controlled by orienting the fibers in a particular way in the epoxy matrix. These compounds are much stronger than titanium, steel or aluminum on a weight basis and have twice the strength-to-weight ratio of fiberglass. For these reasons they can be made far lighter and with a much smaller diameter than either glass or bamboo. Their stiffness-to-weight ratio, which gives them their much-praised casting ease, can greatly exceed that of any other material.

I have heard tales from assorted angling associates about graphite rods, most especially the early production models, shattering upon impact against something like the side of a boat or a protruding rock. In 1975 there were waves of rumors about changing chemical formulas with beefed-up percentages of glass to give graphite more durability. Of course, the more graphite in the stick, the more pronounced the qualities that make it desirable, but the more brittle it is. If you make a graphite mostly of fiberglass you haven't gained a great deal. However, in the summer of 1975 Russ Peak showed me a small rod made with a graphite tip and glass butt that was really fine. It was an experimental model but points to an interesting future for graphite. By this point Russ was getting into graphite rods himself, something he had resisted earlier because of strong doubts about the sensitivity and quality of early blanks. But like everything Russ handles, he was involved with selecting tapers and producing blanks to his very rigid specifications.

There have been so many claims and counterclaims about graphite rods over the past few years since their introduction that it is difficult to make sense of them. Each new model that hits

Keeper ring, Paul Young Para 15

Stripper guide, bamboo rod

Hook keeper, homemade midge rod

Ferrule on custom-made rod

Cross section of six-strip bamboo rod

the market is supposedly the ultimate. The Fenwicks, Orvises, Cortlands, Leonards and so forth have their boosters both inside and outside the manufacturing enclaves.

I have owned and used a number of graphites, including Fenwick, Cortland, Orvis and Shakespeare, and am of very mixed feeling about them. The larger ones over 8 feet which took No. 8 or heavier lines were certainly casting machines. They could heave a line to my 100-foot outer limit as quickly as I had believed possible. But these rods were possessed of little or no grace, something I like even in outsized sticks. For me, in the kinds of fishing I do most, there is a need for some control over the line, especially when in casting, and this is something lacking in the graphites thus far. Casting is very mechanical with them, or at least mechanical in comparison with cane or good glass.

There is also a bit of a myth about the distance possible with them. In the early days some flackish-type outdoor writers were claiming an extra 20 to 25 feet using graphite. For even a journeyman caster it just ain't so. Tournament casters using the new contraptions claim a couple of feet at best. The beginner will find some advantage because of the increased line speed possible with this stiff material. They help to develop the semimythical tight loops that the experts laud. Their big casting advantage comes from a casting smoothness and ease that can help correct sloppy casting traits and make a day of casting a much less tiring process.

Where they really come into their own is in very long rods carrying light lines. Friend Russ Chatham has used a 10½-footer designed for steelheading and raves over its potential. It is as light as his normal 9-foot glass rod and gives him much more line control. At the other end of the spectrum Leonard Wright, Jr., has been toying with a featherlight 9-footer that takes a No. 5 line and is now one of his favorite outfits for his method of caddis fishing.

The lighter graphites I have used were interesting but not compelling. A 7-foot Cortland has been fun to use on smallish creeks since it takes a No. 4 line but can be abused with big flies when necessary and will handle a 60-foot cast without complaining too much. When the serious season for small dry flies comes around, I find a bamboo rod in my hand, but the graphite has been, well, an amusing diversion. Some of the small, very light graphites seem incredibly clubby. They have few of the qualities that one normally associates with tiny tackle and their sole virtue seems in distance casting, something of dubious concern with "toys."

Because of their inherent stiffness the small graphites have problems with the 7X and 8X tippets matched with No. 20 and smaller flies that are now fashionable. They can snap off such ephemeral combinations with startling alacrity.

Even though the prices started dropping in 1975, the $150 general price tag for American graphites seems a bit much. Perhaps in a few years when the state of the graphite art has progressed enough for a genuine diversity of taper and the finish is of top quality, graphites will be worth a major investment. If you are really hot for one now and the $80-or-less Japanese ones aren't your cup of tea, build one out of a blank.

From the perspective of only a couple of years, it is hard to evaluate the true importance of graphites. All the manufacturers are either into or potentially into graphites, so they may become superb tools, but so far there is still a large element of fad in them.

Sometimes I get impatient with myself and others who propose traditionalist arguments against tackle change. There were undoubtedly people like me who believed their greenhearts were superior and would never be replaced by a transitory fashion for six-sided bamboo. But it has to be remembered that it took about two decades from the time that Phillippi made the first split-cane rod until Leonard and others made them into really carefully designed fishing instruments. It took time to incorporate the basic theories and notions of cane into well-tapered rods. It also took a couple of decades before fiberglass rods were developed into the well-thought-out instruments they are today. The vast majority of the early rods were crude, and those who climbed on the glass bandwagon in the late 1940's, throwing away their good cane rods, had reason to regret it.

It always takes time before theory and practice blend in a practical and satisfactory way.

3

Basics of Rod Buying

I

Eight feet long and takes a No. 6 line: the basic rod for fresh-water trout fishing.

Most outdoor writers who deal with tackle hedge the issue of the "all-around rod" and for good reason, since it is really sticking your neck out to suggest the universal casting machine. Nevertheless, this chapter is going to attempt to help you pick your first fly rod—or even the second or third if you've already made dumb choices. There are many factors that must be considered, and the choices can vary incredibly. Otto Teller, a Trout Unlimited director, has fished western Montana for decades, using bamboo rods that are the essence of light East Coast tools. His lines are No. 4's and No. 5's, and his casts are invariably within 25 feet. Without a doubt, he is an excellent angler. At the other extreme, I know Montanans who use 9-footers, carrying No. 9 lines for all their trouting, including small dries, as well as the big muddlers they send sailing 50 feet or more.

It is all compromise, even if you have a dozen rods. It always seems you have to use big flies on a day you have a tiny rod and small flies on a day you hold a telephone pole. As Lucretius says, such is the nature of things.

Let's start at the beginning.

The major factor in choosing a rod is your taste in action, followed by size. Finally, you should consider weight, a factor to which the English, for instance, pay little attention. Unless you are an impulse buyer, a real hazard for the fly-fisherperson, it's best to have a price range in mind before you start. There are adequate, if not good, rods in just about any bracket from $10 to $500, but you don't always get what you pay for. There are some notions of quality that you should know about as you shop, so that comparison of the rods in various categories is possible. I'm going to mention brand names, but certainly in no definitive way. There are too many rods on today's market for anyone except perhaps a marketing expert to know about them all. This is just a representative list of some I am familiar with and that have good qualities.

In the lower end of the scale, say below $25, all that glitters is gold tinsel. Most of the discount-house rods, unless well-known brands like Fenwick, are junkos. They are sluggish, heavy rods that won't give you as much pleasure as headaches. As a rule of thumb, the less expensive a rod, the less fancy it should be. You can't avoid the cheesy metal reel seats on most of those rods, but there are some defensive steps that you can take.

Ferrules are also a danger area. You can't get a rod with a decent metal ferrule these days for much less than $100. Around 1970, when elegant Leonard was still listing ferrules for its fine bamboo rods, they were about $20—which gives you an idea of how much machined joints cost. Stick to the glass-to-glass models that nearly all the reputable manufacturers are using now. The best glass ferrules are those built from the blank itself. A few years back such ferrules could be troublesome, but not any more (unless you get a rare lemon). You get a smoother action with glass than with metal ferrules—especially on cheaper rods. The best glass ferrules are those with thin metal rims, giving added strength and protection. You won't find those on inexpensive models, however.

My advice to someone looking for the best possible rod in this price range would be to get a good blank, such as a Winston, and do it yourself. It isn't very difficult to put together a glass rod if the blank comes equipped with ferrules, and you'll be better off (generally spending $25 on a blank and $5 on fitting) than trying to get a good completed rod for the same amount of cash.

If you insist on a finished rod, one rule of thumb is to get close to one guide per foot of rod. Even manufacturers of the most inexpensive spreads are getting better on this matter. A few years ago, a friend proudly waved his new acquisition in my face—an 8-foot, ten-dollar Thingamajig that had four guides and a tip-top on it. The line slapped around like a clothesline in a hurricane. Except for the really rinky discount stores, you shouldn't encounter this problem any longer—just remember the guide-per-foot motto.

As far as action goes, there isn't much choice in the rods under $25. They are generally what is considered or at least called "progressive action," but that's a little overstated. This rod-design theory, which plagued the glass rodmakers for years and kept them in the dark ages, maintained that the more line you had out, the more the rod should bend. Of course this is true. Whatever kind of rod you use, the more line weight, the deeper the bend, but these "progressive" rods tended to be tippy and sloppy on long casts and heavy on short ones. They should be avoided if possible. Unless you are lucky enough to find something resembling a semiparabolic (which is unlikely in this bracket), settle on a rod that is even-actioned. Even though it isn't materially more difficult to produce inexpensive rods with a nice action, manufacturers seem to believe that their owners are simple-minded people without any sense of quality. Poverty equals nondiscrimination to them.

The market between $25 and $50 is a no-man's-land, consisting of bargains from the $50-plus range and overpriced refugees from the bottom. There are marginal rods, like the Fenwicks, that list for a bit more but can be found at discount prices. Of course, with the economic picture jumping between staggering inflation and depression in the mid-70's, it's hard to make generalizations about prices.

Between $50 and $100 there are lots of nice rods, including Scientific Anglers, Winstons, Walton Powells, Orvis or Leonard glass ones and so on. They can be found in every size and weight imaginable—for every rod taste both "normal" and "perverse." If you stick with the well-known brand names in this bracket, you will do okay until your rod taste develops individual characteristics.

The lesser-known brands can be the best or worst buy. Dick Eggert and I, while semicollegians in Michigan, discovered a rodmaker living along Crooked Lake in the northern part of the state. He was possessed by some utterly wild ideas on rod design, which he patiently described in minute detail. Once we settled him down to work instead of talk, he made for us a pair of lovely, light fly rods for $35 apiece. They are still fine rods and the best buy I found at the time in glass. I have run across other

Standard

Gordon

Half Wells

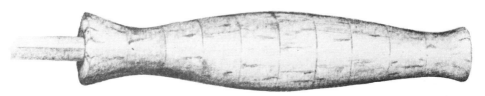

Fishtail

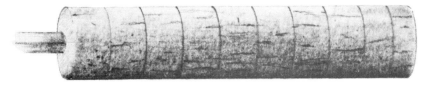

European

Full Wells

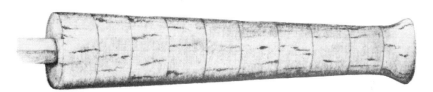

Ritz

Cigar

good buys from conscientious craftsmen who would give you more than your money's worth in comparison to production rods from the supermarket racks. The builders often start with good blanks and lavish loving care in the construction of their rods, to make exactly what you want. However, these artisans scattered around the country can be risky for the novice. They are almost always enthusiastic, charming, seductive fellows who can convince anyone without an arsenal of info that their particular methodology makes the finest pole since Jim Payne died.

A few years back I ran into a fellow on the Gallatin River frantically waving a really strange-looking stick. He saw me staring and came ashore to show off his 5-foot, all-tip, huge-guided thing which he told me had been created by a genius in Wisconsin. It took a No. 7 line and reminded me of a bullwhip. He waited for my comments. I told him noncommittally that it was a nice rod, neglecting to add, "for a light spinning outfit."

There is still all sorts of mysticism surrounding rod action—stuff the beginner, once again, has to be cautious about. Stick with the regular rods unless you know you are getting something better.

But to get back to the $50-plus rods, they should be nice. The finish on them should be smooth and they should have good, sturdy guides. The ferrules should fit well, the reel seat should be of good quality and they should feel right with a line on. No tricky actions, no gimmicks—just a clean rig. The Winston and the Cummins rods fit into this category perfectly. Until the Winston came along, I always recommended Scientific Anglers to rookie friends, but I like the wide variety of actions and the better finish on these newcomers.

Here again, even in this price arena, I recommend glass ferrules. The ferrules take the most stress on a rod. Top-quality metal ones simply cost too much to expect to find them on $50 rods. I think that glass ferrules on glass rods are, at least for now, the best choice.

If I were spending this kind of money, I would want to select from a wide choice of actions and rod handles. Some of the better producers will make various handle styles for you, but there is a wait to get them. It is often worthwhile, since you then get what you really want. To many people, those details aren't important in comparison to the feel of the rod—to others they are very important. Take your choice.

Here is a place for a word about the number of pieces in a rod. There are tons of theories about two-piece versus three-piece. Some say that a ferrule is a dead spot on a rod, referring, of course, to metal ones, and therefore the fewer dead spots, the better the action. Others counter with their thesis that on a three-piece rod the ferrules are not located at the middle, the crucial area for action, and therefore the three-piecer functions better. There has been a minor rash of rods with the single ferrule located toward the butt for this reason. It's very confusing, especially when reality enters the picture. Some of the sweetest rods I've ever felt, including Leonards and Paynes, were three-piecers. I've also tried some cheap three-piecers that were dogs in every respect except barking, feeling as if they were made of a series of contiguous ferrules.

But three-piece rods are handy and worthwhile, preferable to two-piecers if they feel good to you. With glass ferrules, you should give serious consideration to a three-section model. They are harder to find, but the Winston Rod Company, among a few others, has started producing three- and four-piecers for backpacking at no extra cost. I have a four-piece backpacking rod, made for me by master glass smith Russ Peak, that is indistinguishable from a two-piece rod. It is incredibly convenient, fitting in a leather case that attaches to my Big North Face pack wherever I go, whether to Alaska or New York. I never know when I'll meet a fish. It is such a nice rod that I often find myself using it in my home river, the Clark Fork, leaving my good bamboo home.

So you can blend convenience and quality with a little extra effort. Seek and ye shall find.

A word must be inserted about bamboo rods in this category. Though, through a combination of inflation, increasing market and status-oriented greed, cane rod prices have bloated up in the 70's, there are still a few good deals to be found. Here again you have to be cautious. I bought one of these bargains in Denver, took it back to Montana and discovered that you could drive a truck through the cracked glue lines. There was a lot of cashing in during the fly-fishing renaissance, and stuff that shouldn't have been sold at all was billed as the ultimate in elegant equipment, with a price tag fitting the image.

Have someone who knows bamboo go with you if you discover a quaint old shoppe somewhere that happens to have some "excellent quality cane rods for $100 or less." Some of the English imports that mail-order houses brag about are losers. They are base imitations of quality rods with no planning or integrity. Some of them are marketed by reputable English firms that have no real idea what the American angler wants or needs. They are small rods which carry big lines, their awful idea of a dry-fly rod. Another problem is that these rods are sold without extra tips, which —it turns out—are impossible to obtain. I would be very reluctant to purchase any cane rod for which I didn't have a chance to get another tip. To get one of the American rodmakers to build another tip for it will always cost at least as much as the rod itself initially did.

There is a lot of this high-pressure merchandising going on in the 1970's, promoted by companies that should know better. It always seems that when something becomes fashionable, be it stereos, camping equipment or cameras, there are shoddy imitations of the real McCoy to trap the unwary who are without the money or knowledge to avoid the pitfalls. "Glamorous language in a catalog can't hold rotten nodes together," I always say.

Here goes a dangerous generalization that could result in a great deal of flak from the fly-fishing carriage trade. I wouldn't advise the novice to mess around with bamboo rods that sell for $200 or more unless he knows the store owner's sainted mother and could hold her for ransom, if need be, to get his money back. I know too many people who have been badly burned with cane in this price bracket.

Though a bamboo fanatic, I would rather have an excellent glass rod than a mediocre wooden one. You can find excellent synthetics for under $100 but have to be damned lucky to come across good organic rods in this range. To me bamboo comes into its transcendental wonderment only when the rods are outstanding. Bad bamboo is just bad—status aside.

This is not the place to go into high-priced rods or what to look for in them. I wouldn't recommend spending the outrageous asking prices for fine bamboo on your first rod unless you have much more money than sense. Many anglers are sucked into the ultraquality rod mystique by distinguished hustlers waving expensively glamorous offerings. If you are already into that tar pit, it's too late to help. Have a good time.

Now that you know what kind of rod to look for, let's delve into the mysteries of size and line for introductory outfits. There are more generalizations in this section than probably anywhere else in the book, but it can't be helped.

Among the factors involved in wisely choosing a rod is your physical size and strength. If you fool yourself into getting a giant club, telling your friends that you're really a strong devil, you'll be sorry in the long run. In the privacy of your own room, think about what your physical prowess can comfortably handle. Graphite rods and light glass have made the old 6-ounce bamboo a thing of the past, thank goodness. A day on the river with one of them will convince you not to mourn their passing.

You also have to consider the size of the fish you catch and the places you catch them. For most inland trout fishing, you shouldn't have to worry about that, but if you fish for bass in weedy Southern ponds, even if they are only 2-pounders, it is a factor. It takes a rod with oomph to pull a struggling fish out through the lily pads. A light rod, even one capable of tossing hair bugs the required distances, can't cut the mustard for the encumbered fight.

When you are deciding on a rod, the compromise between casting and catching must always be considered. There are lots of sticks that can cast where you want but aren't worth much in the ensuing battle. On the other hand, there are plenty of chunky rods that could haul Moby Dick out of downtown Cleveland but are terrible casters. Some of the Key West tarpon crowd uses, at times, a rod they call the Equalizer, a System 13, on the biggest monsters in the flats. It is truly an awe-inspiring piece of weaponry, the H-bomb of rods, but I wouldn't want to cast it more than a couple of dozen times a day to cruising fish. It could take your shoulder with it after a short time—but then again, you have to feel strong and ambitious to go after 100-pound fish with flies in the first place.

Another very important factor is the length of your casts and the size flies that you work with most often, wherever you fish. If you regularly fish 25-foot streams but cast 100 feet straight up them with a 4/0 Strawberry Blonde, forget the ultralight numbers. If you use average flies for trout fishing and cast average distances, you don't need to consider these things, but I, for one, have no real idea of average flies and average distances. Dick and I can fish together well because we never compete for the same waters. My average cast is around 40 feet and his 20.

Perhaps the best way to clarify this whole business is with some practical examples, sure to raise the hackles (slightly soft!) of every red-blooded prejudiced fly angler in the universe. Let's start out with the basic trout fly rod. Okay, you are going to spend middle season in the Midwest (Michigan, Wisconsin, Minnesota, etc.), fishing middle-sized rivers with middle-sized flies. You are a middle-sized person after middle-sized trout. Get the picture?

Let's use the statistical notion of a standard deviation. No, Harvey, stop giggling, it doesn't mean that. Roughly, a standard deviation is a number which differs from the norm, according to a mathematically defined ratio. I'm going to use the term to mean a one-unit deviation from the formula. Our standard middle trout rod for our middling endeavors will be 7½ or 8 feet for No. 6 line. A standard deviation for it would be one line-weight up or down and 6 inches either way in length. Back to business here.

For the aforesaid person, square in the middle of things, the above rod would be the basic one for casting 40 feet, plus or minus 20, which seems to me to be another relatively standard categorization possible, with flies from 10 to 18, plus or minus two sizes. Getting confused? Well, hold on, it all works out simply.

To repeat, the basic person we're dealing with fishes medium-sized streams (20 to 40 feet wide) with medium-sized flies (10 to 18) for medium-sized trout (12 inches to 2 pounds) with medium-length casts (plus or minus 40 feet). This person (5 feet 8 inches to 6 feet, average build) would probably be happiest with the 7½- to 8-foot rod with a No. 6 line. That's all easy so far, right?

Here come the deviations. If you are small, you might want to go down one unit to a No. 5-line rod that is 7½ or 7 feet. If you are average build, but cast big flies long distances, you might want to go up to an 8½-foot rod using a No. 7 line, especially if your waters are big. There is a kind of organic fluidity about rod length that I'm trying to define, this side of mysticism. If you are bass bugging in weed-choked Florida ponds with 2/0 cork bugs, you might want to go up three standard deviations from the norm—a 9-foot rod taking a No. 9 line. Making sense?

You can follow this scheme up or down. A tiny stream with tiny flies and tiny fish? Go down two units to a 6½-foot rod taking a No. 4 line.

I think this holds, at least for the beginner, in just about any circumstances, even accepting that there will be layers of local bigotry and habit in every region that can cloud the issue. To think about a rod for a given set of circumstances, decide what is the general casting range, the size of the most-used flies, whether the size of the fish is a factor to be considered and if the water conditions (depth, weeds, etc.) will be bothersome. For some conditions, a sinking line that can get wrapped around debris should be fitted on a heavier rod to withstand yanking and pulling.

Another consideration is the wind. Fighting strong gusts with light tackle can be terrible, even though a heavier line has more bulk and resistance. Heavier lines require less false casting and pick up more momentum and energy.

You may have noticed that there has been no mention of rod weight in this chapter—a conscious lack. Any of the good name rods will be properly, or at least semiproperly, balanced and weighted according to size and stiffness. There are exceptions, of course. A 1974 English catalog lists a small trout rod as being 7½ feet and weighing—wow—over 5 ounces. That's extremism! My ideal 8-foot, No. 8-line rod would weigh about 4 ounces in bamboo, a tad less in glass and almost half that in graphite. Shakespeare's 8-foot graphite comes in under 2 ounces. But it's hard to generalize.

Read through the catalogs and see what the general weights are. Some of the better rods tend to be heavy. Orvis, for instance, makes rods that are weighty but very good. Except for special occasions, I don't like bamboo rods weighing more than 4 ounces, so that restricts me to wood rods 8 feet and under. I don't like rods 6 feet and smaller that weigh more than 2 ounces, but these are personal preferences, and I wouldn't want to go to the wall for them. Most of the opinions about weight that noted outdoor writers express in flowing glowing prose come from history and tradition. The novice should learn to discern between things that are good because they are right and tackle fetishes that are adhered to because they have always been adhered to.

4

The History of Rods

There we are, standing on the banks of the Umpqua River with our 8½-foot Powell, equipped with No. 8 quick-sinking line. We know the steelies are up in only this stretch. The fast-moving pool is perfect, but our 75-foot casts with this outfit aren't. The line doesn't get down fast enough, instead whisking along downstream in that nether world between the surface and the bottom where the fish seldom are. We've cast our arms off and, other than a minor skirmish with a boulder, have struck out.

Along comes a fellow holding a crude glass rod, a big Pflueger Medalist and a lead-core, shooting-head line. With one false cast (two would probably bring the heavy head right back into his face) he heaves his bright orange fly across the river. The 30-foot, 400-grain line at the end of its 300 feet of monofilament whizzes out, hits the surface and disappears underneath, sinking much quicker than our commercial line ever could. It plumbs the depths of the pool and is rewarded with a nice fish.

Collapsing on the ground, we curse our fate and our equipment, but we should be grateful for the experience. Besides reducing us to Jello, it brings home a very crucial point about our sport and its development—its dependence on technology.

Most avid readers of the outdoor and fly-fishing publications seem to believe that theory is the key to our sport, rather than equipment. But it just isn't so. Tackle determines the nature and structure of angling; theory just points it in a given direction.

This becomes obvious with a casual glance at the first seventeen centuries of angling history. It must be a casual glance, since hard information for most of that period is nonexistent. But the equipment used between Aelian, a second-century Roman naturalist, and Phillippi, the developer of the split-cane rod, can be guessed at fairly well. This record generally indicates stagnation in rods, tackle and, most likely, practice as well.

From the first hints of sport fishing in Aelian's works, *De animalium natura* ("Nature's Water Animals"), to the mid-nineteenth century, evidently few exciting things happened in either tackle or methods. The Greek poetess, Sappho, an angler, would have felt at home angling with Mid-Victorians even if their moral strictures would have bored her. The flowering of modern angling thought had to wait until equipment expanded its physical possibilities, most especially with the arrival of the cane rod and silk tapered lines.

The rods, more properly poles, used by Aelian, by Sappho, by Dame Juliana Berners, who wrote *The Treatyse of Fysshynge Wyth an Angle* in the mid-fifteenth century, by Izaak Walton two hundred years later, all the way up to Edward Fitzgibbons in the nineteenth century, were probably pretty much alike. The line could only be rolled twice the length of the pole, so these ranged from a hefty 10 feet to a gigantic 20. A 15-foot pole could, at best, handle 25 to 30 feet of line.

Anglers before Walton, including his fly-fishing companion, Charles Cotton, tied light twisted horsetail and mohair lines to the top of their rods. As far back as the fifteenth century, Dame Juliana had recommended in detail how many hairs to use, species by species. One hair for a minnow (the first ultralight angling!), two hairs for bleak and gudgeon, nine hairs for trout, grayling and barbel and fifteen hairs for salmon. These prebambooers were far more subject to the vagaries of weather than we can imagine. Horsehair lines had a very light specific gravity, not able to penetrate much resistance. You had to either dap your fly, a practice still occasionally used in the British Isles, or move up-wind of your fish, making for a lot of maneuvering.

The best way to really understand the difficulties encountered by these early fly anglers is to get hold of a cane pole about 15 feet long, the kind that are used for still perch fishing or winter whitefishing. Tie on an equal length of cuttyhunk or other braided bait-casting line, attach a fly and try your hand in a river. You can learn to handle this rig, but even at its best you will have little in the way of options. Standing there in a light breeze, watching your fly at right angles to your rod, will give you an idea how crucial the modern fly line is to our angling.

To return for a moment to Dame Juliana, she recommends using a piece of equipment that after her was lost to history for a long, long time—the metal ferrule. As far as I have been able to learn, her advocacy of metal ferrules was really unique until the nineteenth century. Almost all rods were joined, until modern times, with beveled joints that were usually wrapped with waxed linen. It isn't that much work to wrap such wooden edges together; in fact, some very traditional English anglers still favor these bindings, especially on salmon rods. A classic young English angler, friend of Dick Eggert, has a favorite salmon rod, a 16-foot Sharpes with spliced ferrules that he binds with—yep—friction tape. The old and the new meet.

Apparently the first mention of "winches" or reels is found in Walton's *Compleat Angler,* so we can safely assume that he and his contemporaries could shorten their lines for dapping and also lengthen them slightly for angling with very favorable gusts. There was no such thing as shooting your line then. Walton had to set his rod down and pull the required amount of line out through the tip-top. It is safe to assume that the first guides and tops were used at this time, mid-seventeenth century, because it is logical that there wouldn't have been any need for guides until there was a reel. Cotton is also the first to mention places where commercial rods were available, so they had progressed somewhat from Juliana's time, when you had to make your own equipment. It's probably correct to guess that reels were commercial products as well. Anyone who is handy at crafting things can make up a fishing "pole" with rudimentary tools, but a reel requires machining, even in its cruder forms (although individuals may have utilized winders that did not contain gears).

The first metal guides, as we know them, didn't appear until the nineteenth century, and even Leonard used the early swivel rings that were wrapped onto the rod. These firm metal guides did not add much to distance casting when they did appear.

The kind of wood used for making rods varied from the earliest times, depending on the length and number of sections or pieces the rod (or pole) contained. Different woods were used for their various strengths and weights. As new woods were discovered in new colonies, anglers utilized their potential in the same way that modern fisherfolk try out developments such as the graphites—the result of space technology. For instance, green-heart and hickory were most often used for tips because they were dense and yet very resilient. Lighter hazel or cedar was used for lower parts because these sections of the rod did not bend as much.

Prior to Walton, as I said, rods were made by the angler or commissioned from a woodworker. Juliana describes how to make a rod disguised as a walking stick from a variety of woods. John Denny, in his 1614 poem, "Secrets of Angling," tells how to select, cut, cure and fashion your own rod. Denny, by the way, was the first to discuss the use of bamboo as a rod material. Of course it was just a piece of bamboo used as a tip, not split cane.

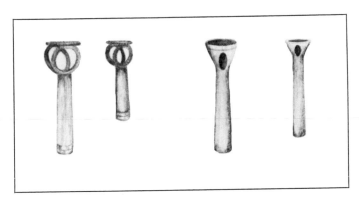

Assortment of turn-of-the-century tip-tops

By the eighteenth century, there were guild craftsmen special-izing in tackle making. These artisans slowly and surely developed the long wooden rod over the next two hundred years. During that period (as horsehair lines began to be waxed), laminated (glued and fitted) sections of hardwoods or hardwood and cane gradually emerged. By the early nineteenth century, some avant-garde English makers were experimenting with "wrent and glued" tip sections. Thus the development of rods came as a slow process and not the apocalyptic development hinted at by some writers. The properties of bamboo were appreciated long before Phillippi put it all together, in the same way that Darwin's, Freud's and Einstein's achievements came largely from earlier sources but took new directions of their own.

Bicycle rod case from near the turn of the century

The ultimate word on the wooden rod came near the end of its heyday—Edward Fitzgibbons's 1847 *Handbook of Angling* describes it as having a solid wood butt, laminated hardwood mid-pieces and a three-section glued bamboo tip. This masterpiece had swivel guides which allowed a braided silk-and-horsehair line to be slowly worked out by primitive false casting. The reel Fitzgibbons favored was a brass single-action one which isn't very different from the ones we use today. His 15-foot outfit was probably capable of handling up to 45 feet of line in a fair breeze.

This was a transitional period. Though the rod could be used to cast the novel dry fly under ideal conditions, the rest of the tackle lagged somewhat behind. Hooks were still forged from needles or hard iron wire, as they had been for hundreds of years, and had to be snelled because the technology to make them eyed as today didn't exist.

The level lines were still very light and crude, and there was no way of making them float other than rapid false casting. Leaders were normally made from twisted horsehair and were not delicate enough to drop a chalk-stream dry fly or nymph on the nose of a wary trout. The theory of upstream fishing could not always be used because the wind hadn't been beaten. The angler in the mid-nineteenth century had to wait for additional tackle developments before he could start dealing with the angling abstractions of Frederick Halford and G. E. M. Skues a few decades off.

A few miles from where I now sit there are some old-timers undoubtedly braving the February chill with tackle closer to Dame Juliana Berners's than to epicurean angler Ernie Schwiebert's. They are using 15-foot cane poles, 15 feet of monofilament, a quill float, a small crude nymph-type fly and probably a maggot. They fish the fast runs and deepish pools of western Montana for whitefish and occasional lunker trout. None of these rigs can be cast, and many have no guides or reels. Others have only a couple of guides and a primitive winder. It is fishing at its most elemental level and the only way some of these faithful know. If a few of our hypermodern anglers who claim such love of tradition were serious, they might try it! These devotees, with their lifetimes of experience, get skunked no more often than we angling technocrats do and probably much less.

You will see, if you check through old catalogs or books compiling old catalogs, that there were wooden rods being made for traditionalists way into the twentieth century. They often utilized modern guides, reel seats and metal ferrules, but the backers of greenheart and other woods believed in them long after the triumph of split cane was supposedly complete.

When Dick Eggert was in Ireland recently, during a camping adventure that featured angling on the road, a revered old rod-maker wanted to make him a 16-foot greenheart rod for about $25. But he blanched a bit when Dick asked about a three-piece 8-footer, which probably would have been the ultimate in snobbery!

It seems that the new becomes the old before the old ever truly disappears.

CANE RODS

Four-strip bamboo end section

Six-strip bamboo end section

Octagonal double-built bamboo rod section, a much-touted but unsuccessful experiment

5

The Great Rod Builders

I

Sam Phillippi, primarily a gunmaker from Easton, Pennsylvania, made the first honest-to-God split-bamboo fly rod in about 1846. Questions of "first" or "second," "real" or "unreal" and such have long been debated. I maintain that the honor for developing the principle of the modern bamboo fly rod must go to Phillippi.

Others, including the London makers, Smyth and Bowness, had been making split-bamboo rod sections from the beginning of the nineteenth century, but there was a real difference between the two types. The English makers were improving on the basic limitations of the traditional solid wood rods by making the fragile tip section more durable and powerful. They did not intrinsically change the nature and substance of the two-thousand-year-old fish pole. These English builders borrowed the techniques of their country's famed longbow makers, whose products were "field-tested" successfully against the French crossbows at the Battle of Agincourt in 1415. The bowmakers laminated sections of wood together into a board and then shaved it into a curving taper. The best English "wrent and glued" bamboo tip sections for the early poles were three-sided, and the hard bamboo surface was on the inside so that the builder could shave his rod to the correct taper after gluing the strips together.

The thin outer surface of the bamboo is the only part of the plant useful in rod building. Hard, silicous fibers run laterally along the length of the grass. In its native surroundings, this surface functions to protect the inside pith from exposure to the high winds which batter coastal China. The shell-like covering permits the stalk to grow up to 100 feet, in spite of violent monsoon gusts. The early British rodmakers did not recognize or appreciate this quality of great strength and resiliency in bamboo. They were caught up in the ancient tenets of rodmaking and saw split bamboo only as an evolutionary improvement on the traditional rod.

Phillippi, however, did recognize the strength and superiority of bamboo and saw it as a way of propelling his fly into the face of the wind. His first rod was probably four-sided, the same number of surfaces that Billie Edwards was to use on his "quads" a century later. Besides being an accomplished gunsmith, Phillippi was a skilled violin maker, and he used the delicate, fine-edged planes and rasps of that craft to miter down the four strips into predetermined tapers. This was a remarkable achievement, permitting him to glue the four parts together with the hard surfaces on the outside, where they would do the most good. There is no simple way of explaining how Phillippi picked up what generations of British builders had missed. His own professions did not equip him for this insight, and there had been no evolutionary trend toward pregluing tapers. Even if Phillippi had been exposed to rod-building technology, which he probably wasn't, he would have had nothing to go on. But there are many ways to account for genius and insight. Perhaps, not being hampered by the tradition-clouded vision of his British counterparts, he was able to see that this was the only way to take true advantage of the strong outside fibers.

Whatever the inspiration, Phillippi's first rod was a wonder, at least a quarter century ahead of its time, leading the way for the vast improvements in tackle that followed. His prototype was short by the standards of the old wooden rods. Most likely it was around 9 feet, weighed ½ pound and was snappy enough to more or less drive the ancient horsehair line through the floppy swivel guides into a mild breeze. Eureka!

Phillippi's marvel was an instant success. He made several for friends and then went into business producing them, with his son Solon, for local anglers. As you see, American anglers at least have always been as gadget-conscious as we are today.

His discovery wasn't covered by any firm patent, and eventually the competition got in on the act. About 1860, a Newark tackle maker named Charles Murphy saw one of Phillippi's rods and recognized it for the gold mine it was. He ran back to his shop, began producing four- to eight-strip rods and sold them at the fastidious Andrew Clark outfittters of New York.

Murphy and New Yorker Edward Mitchell added Madison Avenue–type luxury to Phillippi's brawny backwoods rods, aiming their entire production at wealthy anglers. They produced very elegant models with silver fittings brightly wound with quality silk and put them in fitted satin cases with silver tops and leather covers. These ornate pieces were designed to satisfy the sporting tastes of the East's newly rich—rods for the robber barons. Actually, they were no better fishing tools than old Sam Phillippi's. This was about to change in the second round of bamboo development.

About 1868 an engineer, hunter and woodsman fresh from the Maine wilderness visited New York. This man, Hiram Leonard, was something of a typical nineteenth-century romantic hero, looking for his place in the sun. Raised and educated as a Boston gentleman, he chose the frontier life as a young man. In 1843, he met famed writer and naturalist Henry David Thoreau, who recollected their encounter in *The Maine Woods*. At the time of their meeting, Leonard was already a noted outdoorsman and hunter. The philosophic and reflective Thoreau was delighted with the awesome bearing of this well-born young man, turned Rousseauean noble savage.

By the 1860's, Leonard was one of Maine's frontier dignitaries. Besides his career as a hunter and guide, he had harvested timber and had surveyed much of Maine's wilderness. He was troubled by the contradiction that plagued many of the rugged people who opened the frontiers of America, including Daniel Boone. Having fought against the untrodden wilderness, he had helped turn it into a world that was too civilized for his adventurous nature.

In 1868 Leonard was in his late forties; he and his beloved Maine had become domesticated together. When he took his trip to New York, he was probably looking for a way to make a living that avoided the paradox of being both pimp and lover for unexploited places—a dilemma for many Americans during our history. On this trip Leonard, for the first time, encountered a strange bamboo creation. He looked at the rod, examined it carefully and then played with its action. Right off, he saw possi-

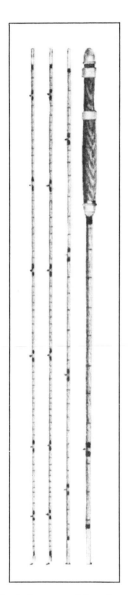

(left) Early Orvis hexagonal bamboo rod with sumac handpiece

(right) Wound sumac handle on a turn-of-the-century Orvis

bilities that this dazzling specimen did not reach and knew he could build something better.

Returning to Bangor, he began experimenting with the tapered strip method and oiled silk lines, which, together with tapered leaders, he had also discovered on his trip to New York. It is known that he made four-, six- and eight-strip rods, while playing endlessly with sections and lengths. For the first battery of finished products, he settled on six-strip rods, from 8½ to 10 feet.

His creations, much simpler than Murphy's deluxe models, were the first genuinely modern fly rods. The ferrules were drawn from nickel silver, soldered into tubes, pieced together and lapped to fit. They had beauty, but that was inherent in the integrated function of the whole rod. He built the handles from cane, as Phillippi had done, and covered them with rattan—a simple yet cozy arrangement. The reel seats were made from finely turned silver bands and caps on silver or wood bases. They held the reel firmly and looked as if their proper place was on fishing equipment, not in a jewelry cabinet. Nothing on a Leonard rod stood out as decoration; every part was hidden within the whole, and the whole had the grace of a fine musical instrument.

Like any fine instrument, Leonards performed. They were much lighter than the rods of any other maker, and the innovative tapers were tuned to the new silk lines instead of to horsehair. Anglers using a Leonard with silk line could develop a perfect balance between line and rod. We now take this simple principle for granted, but in 1868 it was as phenomenal as the telephone was to the first callers.

When Leonard returned to Clark's store with his offerings, the starch-collared salesman must have curled his lip as he drew the new rod from the walnut tube. But when he compared the whispered flick of the Leonard to the heavy-handed recoil of the glittering competition, he probably popped a collar button. There could have been no doubt that this was a superb fly rod. Flyfishing had just come of age.

II

Hiram returned to his Bangor shop to begin to supply Andrew Clark with all the rods he could construct. To do this, he hired wood and metal craftsmen from around Maine's coast. It was quite a gathering, including Fred Thomas, Edward Payne—pioneer rodmaking father of the immortal Jim—and Fred Divine. These men (and Leonard's nephew, Hiram Hawes) formed the hard nucleus of the vintage American rodmakers, by any standards the best the world has known.

Business quickly ripened for the Leonard Rod Company, perhaps becoming a little overripe. In 1876, Leonard agreed to an exclusive sales arrangement with the oldest tackle house in America, William Mills and Son, whose shop in New York dated from the 1830's. For the convenience of this arrangement, Leonard moved his shop to Central Valley, New York, where Leonard rods are still made today, though the company recently moved its headquarters to New Jersey. The move created the first split in the eventual fracture that would send Leonard's original craftsmen into small shops all over the East. First to go was Fred Thomas, who sorely missed his native Maine and returned to Bangor to open his own famous shop.

Thomas rods were made by Fred and then his son Leon for over sixty years. In some respects, they were not as polished as other classic American rods, but they are still cherished for bullish strength and innovative tapers. They began as powerful, stiff rods for Maine lake fishing and were therefore ahead of the dry-fly action rods which began to appear later.

Unlike most other vintage builders, Thomas made several qualities of rods ranging from low-middle-priced ones to those getting top dollar. The Dirigo series was less expensively made than others but featured the advanced Thomas tapers. The most popular Thomas rod was the Special, which combined careful, but not luxurious, workmanship with crisp action. The top line, Browntone, was as elegant and expensive as any rod then sold.

When Thomas left Leonard, Hiram Hawes was hired to fill the opening and, being the boss's nephew, was tutored to take over the shop. About this time, perhaps because of the favoritism shown Hawes, another major schism occurred. Fred Divine left to set up business in Utica.

Divine was a very inventive man, but is not held today in the same misty-eyed reverence as are the other Leonard disciples. He liked gimmicks, such as twisting his rods into full-length spirals, using eight-sided configurations and silk wrapping the entire length of the rod. This made the rods very heavy because he needed to use, say, 10 feet of cane to make an 8-foot spiral rod. Besides this problem, their action was terrible. Nevertheless, in spite of this experimentation, some of his early rods were masterpieces in their own right and, though somewhat wispy of action, were incredibly lovely rods.

Divine died in 1906, but his name was used to make rods for another decade. A friend of mine has a 9-foot Divine salmon rod made about 1915 that he still uses for early-season, high-water trouting. The rod doesn't have much punch left, but it can still handle almost anything that Western rivers require—not bad for a sixty-year-old senior citizen.

Meanwhile, back at the Leonard factory, still another fission was occurring. Ed Payne, Gene Edwards and Hiram Hawes left when Leonard's son, Rubin, took over management of the Central Valley shop. The three dropouts set up the Kosmic Tackle Shop and began to manufacture very high-class rods and some of the most peculiar tackle that has ever been produced. Their partnership didn't last long, and by the first decade of the century, the three split up and began making some of the greatest and most valuable rods ever crafted.

Ed Payne settled in nearby Highland Mills, on a hill almost within sight of the Leonard factory, in a little barn. Ed and his son Jim produced rods from this shop that were, perhaps, the best ever made.

There is a semiapocryphal story that credits Ed Payne with the development of the fast-tipped dry-fly action rod. Even if this is true, the design is not typical of Payne's finer tapers. The action of a typical Payne is substantial, yet light and easy. Jim Payne focused on exceptionally fine fly presentation in a given line weight, moving away from the raw power designs of Thomas. His rods look it too. The cane is fire-toned to a rich brown color, the ferrules are darkened to match and the windings are usually brown with yellow tips. All the hardware on his rods is very tasteful, yet fundamentally functional. The Payne rod represents a school of rodmaking (which later included Gillum among its luminaries) that carried the simple elegance of Leonard to its logical conclusion and not one step beyond.

Jim Payne, weaned on cane and amber glue, is now generally considered to have been the best rodmaker who ever lived. Everett Garrison, whose own skill comes very close, spoke of Payne with a reverence that only another rodmaker can fully appreciate. "Jim," Garrison told me several years ago, "had micrometers for fingers. He could feel that extra one-thousandth of an inch difference without having to pick up a gauge."

Jim Payne's formula for making his living by building rods called for production of one rod per day, per man. Actually, it took about fifteen work hours to build a Payne. Even though these hours were spread over six months, from mitering the cane to the final varnish coat, it doesn't seem like much time for rods which were so incredibly expensive in every era in which they were made. Contemporary custom glass-rod builder Russ Peak spends far more time on his models, for instance. But if you consider Payne's instincts, the talent and, yes, even the genius, his rods were always cheap.

William (W. E.) Edwards, the father of Billie (E. W.) and Gene Edwards, had settled in Bristol, Connecticut, where he built rods in a class with Thomas, with softer actions more suited for the fishing in his area. When he died, sons Billie and Gene parted company, Gene going off to build four-sided rods. Eventually, the Bristol Rod Company bought Edwards's stock and name and marketed Edwards's rods under the Bristol brand for a number of years. Some are marked Bristol-Edwards and others simply Bristol. The company also received some fame for their steel fly rods, which were popular for a few years. The Bristols were decent rods and are often good secondhand buys today.

Hawes is a different story. After breaking away from Kosmic, he set up shop in Central Valley, close to his old Leonard stamping grounds, and built rods well into the 1920's. Few of them are around today. It is said that he didn't maintain consistent production because of family problems. This hypothesis is given some credibility by apologetic notes in the 1917 and 1921 Abercrombie & Fitch catalogs for "long delays" in receiving Hawes rods, asking customers to put in their orders early.

Be that as it may, Hawes rods were the most expensive on the market and certainly some of the best. I saw 7½-foot, 2½-ounce Hawes two years ago and it overwhelmed me. It was, as Ernie Schwiebert would say, a magnificent instrument—deep mahogany brown, with Payne-like fittings colored dark blue and golden windings with brown tips. And the action? It started at the butt swell and moved slowly to the middle, where it picked up a basic rhythm with a No. 4 line that could pace my heart. Utterly erotic! I would consider dumping most of my rods for that dainty Hawes. I have seen other Haweses which were okay but not nearly enough to send me into such rapture. The average customer, looking for a good secondhand rod, needn't concern himself about a Hawes because they very seldom turn up except by some freak of chance and then would bring a staggering price.

Though this era of greatness has vanished, there are still fine rods available. The actions and designs of the masterpieces are incorporated into the specialized fishing tools we use today, both in good glass and in bamboo. These masters, with their incredible workmanship and revolutionary tapers, paved the way for modern fly-rod building, and their instincts, knowledge and brilliance are displayed in every good functional rod you will find.

III

The heyday of the great artisans lasted from the 1930's through the 1950's, at least in a sense directly applicable to our fishing habits. In the East, Jim Payne and Leon Thomas, master builders of the Leonard tradition, made rods for the devotees of the Beaverkill, Battenkill and other classic streams. The Midwest had produced some outstanding third-generation rodmakers of this same school. From Detroit came Paul Young's rods. These fine tools, especially his semiparabolics, are considered by some, such as Arnold Gingrich and Ernie Schwiebert, to be the smoothest-casting rods yet made. Another Michigan builder, Lyle Dickerson, whose specialty was the fast-tipped American dry-fly rod, was also a master. Long-casting Western anglers were salivating over the offerings of other third-generation craftsmen, especially Lew Stoner, founder of the Winston Rod Company, and E. C. Powell.

Frequently, as nonangler Charles Dickens commented, the best of times are also the worst. In general, the 1950's were abysmal times for fly-fishing. The great builders began to disappear from the picture and the infamous spinning reel stepped in, adopted by people who, as Ed Zern once remarked to me, should have known better. With this contrivance, even the rankest amateur could cast a night crawler or tinny spoon a country mile for only $9.95 plus tax. Hordes of neophyte anglers, who never mastered the intricacies of fly-fishing, converted overnight—like natives switching to Christianity upon the appearance of gift-bearing missionaries.

At the same time that spinning caught on, mass-produced fiberglass rods, some designed by misplaced pole-vaulters, whacked the notion of rod quality. The first glass rods that I saw, in the early 50's, as a tyke, were incredible things. The only decent ones, if I remember correctly, were the Silaflexes, which cost boodles of money, $50 for a bass bugger.

But these synthetic rods, with the help of fancy advertising, obliging outdoor writers and glittering wrappings, quickly took over much of the remaining fly-rod business, and by mid-decade all mass-produced rods for the general market were glass. Bamboo production was left in the hands of a few old-timers. The fine walnut and cork reel seats were replaced by cheap metal. The quiet elegance of a Payne or Leonard winding was replaced by tinsel and gold-colored fittings. The American fascination with innovation, which had given us the split-bamboo rod in the nineteenth century, caught up to us with a vengeance in the mid-twentieth.

But despite its general reputation as being rather stodgy, if not reactionary, fly-fishing is quite progressive. While the outdoor magazines blared headlines about this or that whale getting nabbed by smiling Joe Smith with his trusty Zebco, fly-fishing started to undergo a transformation almost as profound as the changes a hundred years before. These changes didn't take place among club members on private waters, but among the young hustling fish catchers and small companies searching for a foothold in the allegedly free market system. Highly specialized, easy-to-maintain synthetic lines came along, finishing silk as the standard. They enabled even the rookie to cast longer distances than ever. Flytiers began creating exact replicas of things never duplicated before. The mayfly was still being copied, but everything in the quiet spring creeks, lakes and windblown tidal flats was also up for grabs on the tier's bench. Only the rods of the master builders could not get better.

There was another, perhaps more basic, reason for the renovation of fly-fishing. As people looked around at our decaying, polluted environment, some of the glitter which surrounded technology began to tarnish. Just as nineteenth-century romantic writers had eulogized the bucolic and the noble savage, the 1960's saw a neoromantic reaction against machinery, which for many people included the spinning reel. Fly-fishing, with its glorious traditions, simple rhythms and organic way of taking fish, became very appealing to people searching for alternatives to the American way of Progress, at least in recreation.

However, after passing through the bumpkin stage, many newcomers were rudely shocked when they searched for good rods.

The mass-produced rug beaters certainly wouldn't do for someone specializing in the sport. Veteran anglers, never impressed by either spinning or glass fly rods, had held on tightly to their caches of fine rods, and they held the hordes of acquisitive newcomers at bay.

After Chiang Kai-chek fled mainland China, with Mao and the Red Army on his heels, the United States became petulant and established the trade embargo on the People's Republic. The world's only ideal cane for bamboo rods is grown in Canton, so American rod builders were left with nothing but their remaining stock. This happened simultaneously with the growing popularity of glass, and custom builders usually had enough of the good cane to keep up with their dwindling market. In the late 60's, the bamboo rod revival began, quickly devouring the remaining supplies. Finally, some sort of trade relations were again established with China, and a little Canton cane found its way across the ocean.

The demand was higher than the supply, however, and most companies had long waiting lists for good cane rods. There are rumors that some top rodmakers stooped to using cane supplies left over by companies that mass-produced cane rods before the glass days. This would certainly lower the quality of a prime blank, but it has never really been substantiated. It is known that the Dunton Company took over the stock of Montague and made varying grades of rods and blanks available before selling out to Thomas and Thomas a few years back. What other things transpired is hard to tell, but they could add up to scorched hands for the unwary buyer. Some cane was coming into this country circuitously through English and Canadian dealers who didn't have the same scruples we did about dealing with the Chinese.

No one ever became rich building fine custom rods. But there has always been a good, steady market for the creations of the master builders, despite the ready availability of good mass-produced rods like South Bend, Heddon and Montague, and prices as high as $75, even during the Great Depression. For the true believer, especially one with a few bucks, nothing could replace the sensitivity and responsiveness of the best. Then, as now, most people were satisfied with their Fenwicks, Berkeleys and Garcias, but for others it had to be a Leonard or Paul Young.

As the renaissance got underway and the literary classics of the sport were rediscovered, the newcomers' appetites for fine tackle were whetted by lyrical descriptions of those old favored Paynes and Leonards. In the mid-60's, the only top-quality rods produced in any quantity were being turned out by the Leonard and Orvis companies, and these, along with the smaller outfits making a few dozen rods a year, were not nearly enough to meet the demands of an exploding market. During the late 60's and early 70's, the value of fine used cane rods skyrocketed, sometimes into the $500 range and once in a while even higher. Many of the rods, especially those handled by secondhand dealers, are now out of sight, costing far more than they are intrinsically worth, both from historical and utilitarian viewpoints.

Of course, not all good bamboo rods sell for that kind of money —only those created by the men considered to be the American master builders. But after the initial buying rush had swept most of the really desirable rods from the market, prices were boosted amazingly on even second- and third-rank ones. In 1975, something as banal as a mass-produced Wright-McGill 8-footer could sell for $75.

This rod mania really began on the day in 1968 that that great craftsman, Jim Payne, died. Many of the devout, who had nurtured the sacred traditions like priests, feared that his passing would just about finish the already declining hundred-year tradition of split-bamboo rods. Nervous anglers began buying up every one of Payne's rods available at Abercrombie & Fitch, his sole retail outlet. Overnight, his rods jumped in value from $150 to $250 and have continued to climb as they become more and more inaccessible.

This bullish market in Paynes was infectious, and prices skyrocketed for rods made by limited-edition builders like Garrison, Hawes, Thomas and Edwards. Tradition-minded anglers began buying up every fine rod they could find. With a nose for a ready-made market, dealers with elegant lists of previously owned rods opened shop soon afterwards.

In the vanguard of this price climb are the Paynes, Gillums, Haweses and Garrisons. They all share a tastefulness and simplicity that even the most determined contemporary builders, trying to cash in on the rod boom, have been unable to touch.

The highest prices, those from $500 upwards, are usually paid for 8-foot and smaller two-piece rods, currently the high fashion for trout. The old-time favorite, the three-piece 9-footer, is no longer in much demand as a rod to fish with and will sell for $200 less, provided it isn't a particularly beautiful, master-built rod.

The master builders had never produced a lot of rods in their custom shop. Ev Garrison, whose products are unsurpassed in simplicity and beauty, made only some 800 rods in his forty-year career. Actually, he was an engineer. Since many bamboo rods are heir to breakage, both naturally and unnaturally, it's easy to see why the scramble for classic bamboos became a stampede. The $25 Payne found in someone's basement is like the 25-cent first edition of *Alice in Wonderland*—very rare, but surely not unheard of. With heightened competition between dealers scouring the country and a demand far outdistancing the supply, we are in our current fine-rod stew.

6

Buying a Fine Cane Rod

I

Any logical person primarily interested in fishing should be convinced after reading this far that there is no reason to own a bamboo rod. Glass rods are often sturdier, far less expensive, available in just about every action, look fine and are much less difficult to maintain. Graphite rods are more powerful than wooden ones, a lot lighter and can handle a larger variety of line weights easily.

But to try to argue this with a large number of fly-fishermen is like trying to convince a couple in love that their relationship should be platonic. Let's be realistic. The passions that bamboo inspires are deeper than the Yellowstone and faster than the Madison. Again like lovers, they are frequently beyond good sense—sometimes without any sense at all. It is often an "either-or" situation. Anglers are either turned on by bamboo or they couldn't care less about it. No amount of arguing or fussing will make a bit of difference.

A friend of mine, Jan Konigsberg, spent two years in Missoula watching me go through literally dozens of rods. He was always satisfied with a 7½-foot Peak and a Scientific Angler System 8 for his fishing, both in Montana and Alaska. Obligingly, he would shake my fine bamboo wands, nod and go back to glass. Then one day I showed him my Paul Young Para 15, the 8-foot semiparabolic I've spoken of earlier. He tried it out for a bit on the lawn, came in the house with eyes all moist and tender and started offering me mounds of things for it. The Para 15 was the only bamboo rod that ever excited him. But that's the way it goes with wood, ranging from fanatic friends of mine who act as if venereal disease is contracted by handling glass rods, to Dave Harriman, my fish-raising landlord, who switched contentedly from bamboo to glass years ago. It takes all kinds, as they say.

In this age of synthetics, sound knowledge about bamboo is difficult to come by, even since its comeback. Information from the catalogs is usually very sketchy and not at all objective. The old books are often just that—old.

There is the additional problem that high prices and scarcity have caused secondhand prices to grow enormously. I never saw a secondhand rod officially for sale in a store until the late 60's. It was a Payne in Abercrombie's in New York. These days just about every fly shop in America has at least a few, and not very many dealers can honestly vouch for their condition and quality.

Unlike gun collectors, rod collectors covet rods which are usable. The top money paid for Paynes, for example, goes for the 6- and 7-foot models. Not only is this size most popular today, but it is by far the rarest, since the craftsmen worked mostly in a period when longer rods were in vogue. Certainly there are some specialized collectors, but the generalist dominates the market, often trying to get one fishing rod from each of the big-time builders. There are now people specializing in Leonard and Orvis rods, much like collectors of Winchester and Remington firearms. I suspect that this is, at least in mentality, a spillover from the gun world.

Speculation in this unstable market, except by experts, is a good way to get stung. A change in ferrules, windings or reel seat can wipe out a rod's value to the collector, but not necessarily to the appreciative angler. Some of the rods represented as one thing are really something else, and counterfeits can be very difficult to detect.

All in all, this fascinating world of used quality rods is a very interesting playground, but hazardous.

II

As you might have guessed by now, I am a secondhand addict. Junk stores, antique shops and pawn houses draw me like magnets. Upon visiting a new city or revisiting an old one, my first stops will be places where all sorts of used stuff is sold. The things we have to sell, hock and trade are often nicer than the things we keep. There are usually nooks and crannies in secondhand stores where one will sometimes find the real thing, while shops with new items are getting more regimented and plastic.

Look through the most elegant tackle catalogs. What do you see? Mostly the same things you see in all catalogs. Some of the reels, fly boxes, and leader wallets may be nice, but still. . . . The surprise of finding an old rod that turns out to be, under seventeen layers of dust, attractive and usable can be more rewarding than buying a new Orvis. Seeing an old metal leader case, as I did in Denver, that turns out to be a Kosmic made by the first Payne, Edward, after he split off from Leonard, is more delightful than having the best new cases.

All this is a roundabout way of saying that you shouldn't forsake the secondhand stores in your neighborhood. Unless I've beaten you to it, you may find a usable rod there, especially today when more people are fly-fishing with decent tackle. But maybe there are two kinds of people—those who buy things new and those who buy them used. Guarantees and shiny finishes are a requisite for many people, and I think that is why they get junky stuff at times. Is a $200 used fly rod better than a $200 new one? My answer would have to be—potentially! I'm not hedging. It's just that with a bit of luck you can get a superb bamboo stick for $200 secondhand, and what you get new for your $200 is more or less fixed by the current market value.

By the mid-1970's, despite a recession, the prices of bamboo rods are high. At this writing Orvis was just under and Leonard just over $300, with most other makers in the neighborhood. Even Phillipson, never considered a top-of-the-line premium rod, is sailing over the $200 mark. Many anglers are grumbling about the prices and sticking with their $50-to-$100 good glass rods. It seems that these cane-rod companies can sell every rod they make, so they keep the prices going up and up.

The secondhand dealers are also capitalizing on the stratospheric prices. Adding to the phenomena are those greedy anglers hoarding more rods than they could use in three lifetimes. Though it is nearly impossible to find anyone discounting good new bamboo rods, it is still possible to find bargains in used stuff with patience and knowledge.

The market for such things is as sloppy as a fifty-year-old wet-fly rod. Since I started writing about bamboo rods, many people have come up to me brandishing rods they described as invaluable—heirlooms which they would reluctantly part with for only . . . $300. These heirlooms almost invariably turn out to be 9-foot, three-piece Wright-McGills or Montagues reasonably worth, considering use value, not more than $25 to someone looking for a curiosity. But balancing the hordes who think that every bamboo wand is invaluable are generous people who will share their stash of good rods with other anglers for a deserving price. I have run across dozens of stories of young fisherfolk meeting a veteran fly tosser streamside, chatting for a while and having the older person offer him a rod at a fair price. Such is the true stuff of angling.

There are also endless stories of nice or good rods picked up in secondhand stores around the country, even in unlikely places like the Plains States. I once saw an Orvis for sale for $50 in Kansas. I had no use for that big 8½-footer, but it would have been fine for someone, and I'll bet it had an interesting story behind it. Generally, however, I would be cautious before throwing scads of money at a used-rod dealer—most are scrupulous about their stuff, but some aren't. There is a vast difference between what they have invested in a rod and their retail price, so be careful with both your purchases and your trade-ins. You may avoid this middleman cost by beating them to an estate sale, watching the newspapers and so on. If you do find what you want from a used dealer, don't be afraid to bargain with him, no matter how elegant he appears.

The used-rod market is a very touchy place, with few sources for the buyer to study in order to beware of bad deals. Even the most supposedly reputable dealers can be a hazard to your economic health.

I bought, via the mail, a three-piece 7½-foot Leonard for $200, a decent price for a new rod in 1971—$25 less than retail list. When the rod arrived, it looked new—clean and very crispy. I let it sit for a few weeks while I used various other rods. Then I took it to the Bitterroot one fine summer day and it cast nicely. After an hour I looked up and saw the tip pointing halfway around at me, one God-awful set. The rod was obviously not new, I decided, but reconditioned. The other tip immediately set, too, but not quite as badly. Without a doubt, the rod was worth at least $50 less than I paid for it.

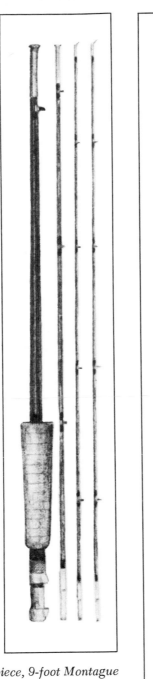

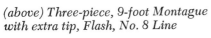

(above) Three-piece, 9-foot Montague with extra tip, Flash, No. 8 Line

(right) Cortland 8½-foot Pro Crest rod

In another case with a secondhand dealer, I was sent a $125 rod represented as an 8-foot, Paul Young dry-fly special, a three-piecer taking a No. 5 line. It was supposedly a lesser-known Young. Dick Eggert happened to be over the night it arrived. We looked at the tippy rod with its dark bamboo suspiciously. It wasn't like any Young we had ever seen—no parabolic action, no mottled wood, no underlying power, just a plain dry-fly rod. We called the dealer, who admitted, after a bit of banter, that it was a rod that Paul Young had put up from a Heddon stick back in the old days, before he designed his own. It was a Heddon in all respects except that Young had put on the guides and reel seat, allowing the dealer to charge three times its value.

There are some basic considerations for anyone getting into used bamboo rods to look out for—precautions that will help prevent that sinking feeling when a newly acquired secondhander snaps the first day out.

The two main things to think about in any rod are utility and quality. It doesn't make any difference if that luscious Thomas or Winston is sublimely made or has never been touched by human hands. If it won't fish, forget it. Some of the best rodmakers in the country made rods that are utterly useless by today's standards.

One of the first matters to insist upon, whether you buy by mail or in person, is the right to test and return it if dissatisfied. Take it out on the grass or water and cast the way you normally fish. Since the word was passed around a few years ago about the importance of casting a rod before purchase, most shops keep a box of lined reels ready. But sometimes this can be tricky too. The Streamside Angler Shop in Missoula is always ready for the test caster to work out along the Clark Fork. However, the shop is located on a man-made bank about 25 feet above a channel of the river. Casters will almost invariably attempt to heave across to the other bank below, a distance of about 75 feet. It isn't very hard to cast that distance, especially when you're casting some of it downhill, but what does it tell you about the rod? Very little. I've seen scads of people standing around with rods under 7½ feet in their hands trying for that lower bank. A real macho thing develops when a few anglers get together on that high bank, trying to outdo each other. I fear, in spite of the best intentions of owner Rich Anderson, some rods are bought merely because they can handle 75 feet of line, as if that were a normal distance for a little stick. The same sort of thing happens in many other places. Unless you are after a steelhead rod, distance is the last thing you should be concerned about.

You are going to have to live with the rod you buy, so be sure that its style, action and distance capabilities are what you are looking for. Once these basic conditions are out of the way, begin to check out the quality. If it can't do your casting job, further tests are useless—unless you can afford dream fodder.

See what general shape the rod is in, looking very carefully for imperfections, which become quickly apparent with experience. While the rod is still together for casting, sight down the guides to see if it has taken a set or bend. You should be able to see clearly through the tip-top and follow the diminishing size from the big bottom stripper to the top.

The reason for a set is fairly simple. A rod will normally recover from a bend in any direction and return to its straight form, but when a rod, from any structural or handling defect, stretches the fibers on one side, a set occurs. Changes in a glue line also occasionally cause sets. In most cases, it doesn't mean that the rod is about to crack or that casting will be impaired, but it is a sign of a problem. Money should be deducted from the price to compensate for a set, and they can be wonderful bargaining points. Like many other anglers, a set offends me to greater and lesser degrees depending on how bad it is and how badly I want the particular rod. Sometimes sets can be successfully repaired, but this does not always work over the long haul. See the next chapter, "Rod Repairs," for some more information about sets and their cures.

Next, holding the rod horizontally, wiggle fairly softly, listening and feeling for ferrule weakness. If you feel a clicking in the handle, go carefully over each ferrule to make sure they are snug and try again. Some people seem to have a greater awareness of slight joint clicks than others. You might want to bring along a sensitive friend. If the click persists despite the tightening, it means that the ferrule fit itself is loose or the bonding between the wood and metal is not what it should be. It could also be an ominous sign of really big trouble in the composition of the cane.

Now take the rod down, with your left hand on the male ferrule and your right hand on the cane. Pull as evenly and straightly as possible. If the ferrules are of good quality and fit correctly, you should hear a pop as they separate. Loose ferrules are a problem, but a bigger danger is bonding that isn't tight. A symptom of this is a broken winding on a ferrule. When the clicking sound comes from metal against wood, it means a repair job for sure, as the wear can break down a rod quickly under rugged casting. The rubbing contact may dig deeply into the bamboo, weakening it enough to allow an extra long cast or a nice-sized fish to finish the rod.

After taking care of this detail, begin checking out the guides for wear, especially if it is an older rod with agate or synthetic agatine stripping or tip guides. These guides were considered much smoother than metal ones in their day. To find out if these usually transparent red guides are cracked, hold them up to a light and look for hairline cracks while moving them from side to side. At certain angles the breaks will appear like prisms. Cracks in agate or other gem-type fittings can set up a fly line incredibly fast—making short work of a new Cortland 444 in an afternoon. Replacements are hard to find; most anglers concerned with the use value of a rod will replace cracked agate or agatine guides with standard snake guides.

Now check over the windings. Is the varnish on them cracked or peeled, or is it tight and tidy? Guides will eventually wear through the winds on a much-used rod. Good winding material, traditionally silk, should be very fine, each wrapping barely visible. Also check to make sure all the winds are identical and that some-one has not added one or two of their own. If you know a hard-core rod buff, check out what the original wrappings on the brand were. Nonoriginal wrappings, a very common alteration, detract from a good rod's value.

Now we get into the hardest part—the cane itself. Bamboo rods are made from four, five, six or more sections of mitered cane strips. Most rods have six sections, though for a while Gene Edwards made four-strippers and Nat Uslan made five-strip ones. These strips are glued together, forming the multisided construction of the completed rod.

Before World War II and the invasion of the Orvis Impregnated, which started a major trend, all rods were made with natural glues, basically manufactured from horse hooves and amber but with other special and often secret ingredients that the makers did not talk about. This glue was applied hot and allowed to cool dry, providing a firm but malleable bond. The big problem with these concoctions was their sensitivity to a number of elements, including extreme heat, cold and, most especially, moisture. But natural glues often hold up as well, with the proper care, as the modern epoxy-type compounds. John Voelker, who writes wonderful fishing books under the pen name Robert Traver, once showed me a seventy-year-old Leonard that was still strong and firm despite being fished hard.

Any old rod made with natural glues, regardless of quality, can have split or seamed joints. To check for open seams, look down each section along the point ridges. Go very cautiously, because minor seamed joints are hard to detect. Look for cracks in the varnish over the seams, which indicate an open joint. Also beware of dark-colored ridges between lighter-colored bamboo, which indicate a seamed joint. A really sound rod should have completely closed joints all the way along its length. A rod that has seamed joints can still be useful, but on the other hand, it could split open at any time. A rod that has a really open joint is practically useless unless repaired by a professional—an expensive operation.

Move on down to the handle. Has it been badly abused or obviously modified? If it's been altered, deduct a small amount from the price you will pay, but don't fret. Handles are easy to replace, so don't throw the baby out with the bath water. If the handle is in poor shape, requiring modification or rebuilding, subtract a greater amount from your offer, enough to pay for the repairs.

How about the reel seat? Sliding band seats, popular on light rods, have slim tolerances for the various thicknesses of reel footings. It is a good idea to bring along the reel you intend to use with the rod to make sure it will fit comfortably. In the past I have used tape to build up reels to keep them on the rod, but it's really a hassle, especially when your reel shoots off into the water with a cast. If the seat uses a screw lock, be sure that the threads are still sound; otherwise the reel will loosen while fishing. Sometimes bad threads will cause your reel to jam on the rod. One cheap steelhead rod I hastily put together was so shoddy that I had to use a hammer and screwdriver to get a damn reel off. A little dirt on cheap seats can cause great frustrations, even if you are not the hair-tearing type.

It's time to consider the whole rod as a unit. How well was it made? This consideration has more to do with the price of a used rod than either condition or utility—a rather sad state of affairs. A Jim Payne in barely recognizable condition will fetch four times

Reel seat, screw lock

Reel seat, Cortland Pro Crest, all metal

Reel seat for late-model Paul Young 7½-foot Perfectionist rod

the price of a mint Montague. But is the Payne really a Payne? These fine rods were made to a startlingly high standard, and some purporting to be Paynes aren't. Just because it is stamped on the butt cap doesn't necessarily mean it's so. Like any other thing where money is involved, a lot of hustling is going on.

The first thing to look for in a quality rod is the fittings. Most good makers stamped their names on the butt caps or barrel of the reel seat, rather than writing along the butt with black ink. Check for a name here and also for sharp precision machine marks along the edges of the rings, caps and checks. Good makers have always lathe-turned their fittings, while lesser rods have less-defined stamp-cut fittings.

The ferrules should also be machine-turned, rather than mass-produced with a stamp. The end plug on the male should be tight and flat against the bottom of the female. The shoulder on the male ferrule should have a pronounced machine cutting and, like everything else, look neat. The female joint should have a metal plug inside, a soldered disc called a watercheck, which snugs against the male. This all sounds terribly erotic—and probably is! All the metal parts on a fine rod should be made from nickel or German silver, except a few aluminum experimental ferrules made to be ultralight on some rods produced during the midge days of the early 60's. These experimental ferrules don't hold glue and can't be pinned—they should be immediately replaced.

Most cheap rods use hardware of chrome-plated brass, easy to tell from the quality dressings. Chrome is bright and shiny, while silver is velvety and more subdued when new or polished. An old rod with silver fittings should be naturally somewhat tarnished or discolored.

Each of the good builders had characteristic ways of assembling his strips to space the nodes according to the way he thought best and most practical. Payne spiraled the nodes around each section so that no two nodes were ever together at the same place on a finished section. Leonard, on the other hand, deliberately placed three nodes at the same height but always made sure that a clear strip of cane separated each one. Paul Young would place two nodes opposite one another and spiral up the rod with this sequence.

Aside from these peculiarities, which are apparent on every fine rod to the discerning, the basic thing to remember is that each builder had an exact method of spacing nodes. Look for the method and make sure it is consistent throughout the rod. If you see two or three nodes lumped against each other, you can bet that it was not carefully made, regardless of who the seller claims the maker was. If the node system appears haphazard and without set rhythms, it is a dead giveaway of an inexpensive rod. Cane has always been the essence of a good rod, so you should pay more attention to it than anything else.

Sometimes the impregnation process can hide a multitude of sins. The process was allegedly discovered by Ev Garrison before World War II, but he discarded it in favor of traditional methods because he believed impregnated rods lost their delicacy and were too heavy. A few years later Orvis picked up the im-

65

Elk-horn reel seat made by Jeff Johnson, Missoula

Reel seat on Scott Power Ply glass rod

Reel seat used on Hardy Hollokona and Hollolight rods

Reel seat, 7½-foot Winston rod

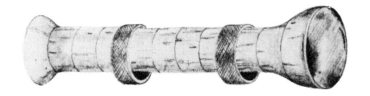

Reel seat, Orvis DeLuxe, silver reel bands

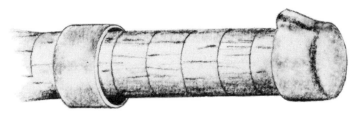

Reel seat, Scott Power Ply pack rod

Reel seat, all cork with rings, custom-made

Reel seat, custom-made walnut

pregnation idea. They developed a process of soaking the rod blanks in special hot glues, usually Bakelite resins. Other manufacturers use a similar process with epoxy-type glues. The process puts a protective finish in the rod, not just on it, adding further protection from moisture and abuse. The idea caught on then, and many builders began using similar impregnation techniques. It surely strengthens a rod, but also can make it feel full and lifeless, as the shampoo commercials say. Sloppy craftsmanship can be covered by impregnation, so look them over extra carefully. You have to weigh strength and durability against the traditional attractions of bamboo's delicacy and feel.

I should say a word here about refinished and repaired rods. Most people who own good rods have enough sense to have them refinished when they need it by very competent artisans. Therefore it is difficult for all but the most experienced to tell repair jobs from original finishes. If the varnish is light and smooth, without lumps or hairs, it will probably last you as long as can be expected and you needn't be overly concerned whether the rod is wearing its first suit or not. However, don't be afraid to decide if the emperor is wearing clothes or not! Varnish cracks can let moisture seep in and cause long-range problems on rods with animal glues. On the other hand, all used rods will show a little cracked varnish, so you'll have to use your discretion.

Many older rods, even those with kindly owners, will have clear silk bindings here or there. These were put on to compress the cane where it began to separate or fracture. Bindings along the butt section usually do not affect the action of a rod, and you have to have a very sensitive touch to feel a small wrap binding even on a delicate tip section. Bindings often drastically reduce the price of a secondhand rod but most likely will not affect its usefulness. Many rod shoppers recoil at the sight of these splints, going along with the cult of the "perpetual virgin" in this society. One of the old Leonard factory repairmen once remarked that such binds were "service ribbons," adding that "if a good rod doesn't have one now it most likely will someday." Of course, I have seen sloppy silk or nylon bindings covering half a rod section, and you should watch out for them. These windings should be carefully and discreetly accomplished. Many rod dealers will send such a rod in and get a section replaced or completely refinished, knowing that they can get a lot more money for it. Some buyers are looking for perfection rather than use and will pay top dollars for a "perfect" rod.

All these considerations should be taken into account by the buyer and the seller in figuring out a fair price. However, you can't expect all dealers to adopt this logic. Buyer beware and all that rot. If you find a useful quality rod that needs some work, subtract the amount of money and anxiety it will cost to have it revitalized. A good rebuilding job these days will cost between $60 and $100 or even more, depending on the care it needs. Getting a section replaced can set you back $100, so prepare yourself if it's necessary. It is always wise to send a repair job to the shop during the slow winter months, rather than the tip-busting trout season.

The following list is not comprehensive and certainly is not a definitive price index. The fluctuations of the rod market have been incredible recently, and it can be confusing. In the past few years, I have developed some ideas on buying, where bargains may be found and what to watch out for. I hope the dealers won't read this and jack the prices up on the bargains. Undoubtedly, you can make money buying a Gillum or Payne low and selling it high, but this isn't a book for the recreational Wall Streeter. All rods are described with their use value.

There are also bargains to be found in off-brand bamboo rods sometimes—but again, it is dangerous. Some of the better-known outfits, like Thomas, made rods for Abercrombie & Fitch and others. Heddon made some nice rods for Folsom and even Montgomery Ward, and so on. Look for identification marks like ferrules, windings and reel seats, a skill that will take time to learn.

USED BAMBOO ROD LIST

Horrocks-Ibbotson—$25 down. Low-priced rod. Some of the smaller ones weren't bad, but most commonly found is the three-piece 9-footer—let sleeping dogs lie!

Dunton—$25 to $150. Wide range of prices for a wide range of rods made by the company that took over Montague's bamboo stock. Thomas and Thomas took Dunton over in the 1970's. Dunton sold a wide variety of rods and blanks that covered the whole spectrum of rod quality, from excellent custom ones at the top of their line to some—*echh*—at the bottom. Not great rods, but possibly a bargain area if you find a good one cheap. They had some cheesy ferrules and fittings near the rear of their list, but used Super Z's, etc., on better models.

69

South Bend—$50. Bargain alert! You can sometimes find choice light rods for under $50. They were mass-produced and very popular in the 30's and 40's. There are plenty of these usable rods floating around with acceptable ferrules and reel seats. The 7½-footer is a nice dry-fly rod, with distinctive gold-colored cane.

Heddon—$50 up. Another possible bargain area. They turned out a huge line of rods. The upper end of the line—Presidential and the like—were handmade and comparable in price and quality to outstanding rods of the time. Can be expensive, but you may find some good lower-line Heddons at reasonable prices. Heddon made many rods that were retailed as private brands. These dark-colored rods often have quick tips and can be good dry-fly rods.

Montague—$50. This is a possible bargain area. Some Montagues are very nice, including light ones and salmon types. There is a wide variety of rods, prices and quality. William Mills, who retailed Leonard, sold a Montague salmon rod, a big endorsement.

Farlow—Under $65. Some like 'em, but I'm wary of these rods, many of which were made by the English for our waters. Their design seems funny, and the Farlows built for English consumption seem much better.

Cortland—Under $75. Run-of-the-mill English import, impregnated and a bit stiffish. An okay rod, but not at all special, unless at a bargain price.

Uslan—$75. Many of these five-strippers are terribly woody, but I had an 8-footer that was an outstanding rod. Be sure to check the action carefully, as many are very clubby. Al McClane raved about them in his *American Angler*.

Constable—$75. Like the Farlows, these rods make me uneasy, although other knowledgeable people are satisfied with them. They are also a British import for the burgeoning American rod market.

Sharpes—$75. Another English rod for the Yanks—see Cortland. The impregnated ones usually have some saving graces.

Phillipson—$100 down. Bill Phillipson, who seems to have been influenced by Granger, made rods for a long time, and many of the older ones are very nice. The recent ones are impregnated, but only so-so. Watch out for ferrules, loose seams, etc.

ROD TAPERS

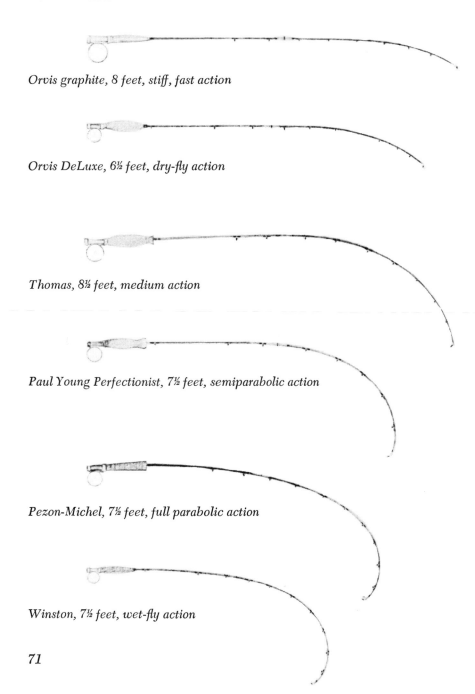

Orvis graphite, 8 feet, stiff, fast action

Orvis DeLuxe, 6½ feet, dry-fly action

Thomas, 8½ feet, medium action

Paul Young Perfectionist, 7½ feet, semiparabolic action

Pezon-Michel, 7½ feet, full parabolic action

Winston, 7½ feet, wet-fly action

71

Cross—Vicinity of $100. Pretty good rods, but tend to be heavy and very powerful. Butt and midsections were Double Built, a Cross trademark. Many of their designs are awkward for my taste, but there are some Cross aficionados among salmon anglers who like the power, if not the glory.

Pezon & Michel—$100. Nice French rods, sometimes called Ritzes, since Charlie designed them for his parabolic tastes. They are pretty rods for $100 if you can adapt to the necessary casting techniques. I suspect they have some breakage problems. Keep in mind that the big ones are heavy and can be exhausting. A slow sense of timing has to be worked out.

Granger—From $125 way down. Possible bargains, but full of dangers at a variety of prices. Some of the original light Goodwin Grangers were charming rods, but sometimes a little bottom-heavy. However, Wright & McGill later took over the Denver Company and produced some not-very-valuable sticks that have toasted fingers too quick to the wallet—fingers thought to be grabbing at originals.

Paul Young—$80 up and up. Lovely dark rich bamboo rods, semi-impregnated and semiparabolic, offered from the famous midge at 6 feet 3 inches to some Godzilla-sized models. They will sell from $150 skyward when constructed by the factory, but there are some real bargains ($100 range) for rods made from sticks bought from Young and put up by the buyer. The small ones are superb casters, but the big ones, over 5 ounces, take a lot of strength.

Hardy—$100 up. Trillions of these rods have been imported and some of them are utterly useless for the sensible modern angler. They do look pretty, all dressed like the proper English rods they are. Some Hardys, made for the English market, are good buys at $125; light models like the Marvel and Phantom. The big ones are usually too woody and ill-conceived for our way of fishing. Watch out for current ones that are skimpy; they are no bargain at $175. Hardy rods are loved by the British—even the clubbish ones. Many Englishmen consider them the best rods in the world.

Orvis—$100 up. The floodgates really burst open at the mention of this venerable company, which got heavily into the rod market with impregnated designs at the end of World War II. They have made innumerable models, including a few even they don't remember. Some of the newer ones don't hold up that well, despite the traditional claims that Orvises were built to last, not so much to cast. Some of them are heavy, but you have a wide choice and some are really nice rods. Don't pay more than $150 for any model, despite their inflated modern price tags. Take your time about picking one and try the factory in Manchester, Vermont. They sometimes have secondhand ones available.

Winston—$150 up. Few bargains in Winstons unless priced under $150. Although some have been known to break or set quickly, Winston is a fine Western rod, especially in the 8- to 8½-foot range for casting big dries a long way. Some Winston steelhead rods are also excellent and have a hard-core following on the West Coast.

Thomas and Thomas—$150. This is a newcomer capitalizing on the rod renaissance. They offer a long list of impregnated and regular rods for nearly every taste. Some are nice, others bow-wowish, so don't pay a lot unless you know that it is exactly what you need.

Dickerson—$150. These very pretty and classic rods, made by a Michigander, are usually fast-tipped. They are fine traditional dry-fly rods, a bargain if you like the feel, and as close to the East Coast tradition as many get.

E. C. Powell—$150. Powell's powerful rods were most famous, but he made all actions. The dark-colored bamboo is coveted by West Coasters, and he specialized in heat-treating the wood. His Tournament rods are popular with steelheaders.

Vom Hofe—$150. This is a possible high-priced bargain area for the dry-fly enthusiast. This fine reel-making company also made rods from heavy trout to salmon, but they are fairly hard to find.

Leonard—$150 up—and up. The oldest and one of the best. For a usable, modern-action Leonard, you should go to about $225 if it's in good shape. Check the tips carefully and try to get it dated. Beware of the old, soft Leonards.

Edwards—$200 down. The early Edwardses were six sections and in a class with Thomas and Leonard. Edwards's later rods were made with four sections and are not considered to be as nice as the earlier ones. Watch out for the Bristol Edwards, an okay rod—not worth as much but a possible bargain for the knowledgeable.

Thomas—$200 up. A very traditional, usually powerful rod from Maine. Some were heavy and others too tippy for most people. At $200 and over, the high-level Browntone and Special are not great bargains. The Dirigo, at the bottom of the list, is sometimes more reasonably priced. Thomas made the rods in slow, medium and fast actions and made many models, including varying grades of quality.

Payne—$300. The ultimate in both price and quality. Check them out very carefully before spending the $500 or more that dealers will want. I don't think one Payne is worth the price of two other fine rods, everything considered, but keep looking . . . one enchanted evening. At $300 they are a good deal, in intermediate or smaller sizes, but rumors are that a few counterfeited ones are floating around, so be careful. His parabolic rods are especially nice for modern tastes.

Garrison—$400. Another of the truly greats. Ev Garrison's rods, made with utter simplicity and cleanness of design, are bringing minor fortunes. Collectors are very hot for the light-brown, medium-action or tippy rods. They seem to grow on you with time. There is little chance of getting one for less than $400; there were less than a thousand ever made.

Gillum—$400. Another big-dollar rod, made by a man who paid more attention to the cane he used than anyone else. He worked for Payne and was greatly influenced by him and Leonard. Very fine rods, but hard to find and ultraexpensive.

Hawes—$400 up. Big bucks will be asked for these fine Payne-like rods. They were mostly made after the turn of the century and are very rare. Hawes was one of the original Leonard people and he did very delicate, exact work.

7

Rod Repairs

Even the simplest things have problems at times. No matter how carefully you watch over the health of your rods, if you use them hard, sooner or later they are going to get injuries or illnesses of one type or another.

Actually, it is amazing that rods, especially bamboo ones, get into trouble as seldom as they do. They are just wood, glue and cork and are called on to perform year after year under a great deal of pressure and stress. It is a tribute to the builder's craft that we use and often abuse them season after season with only a minimum amount of complaint from their innards.

Fixing cane rods is an easy process if you have lots of experience and a most difficult task for the beginner. This is a warning. Most of the mend-it-at-home recommendations are potentially dangerous and can destroy a $250 rod. I suggest sending your rods off to a reputable shop for all but the most elementary jobs, such as wrapping guides and ferrules, even though rod hospitals are now charging as much as hospitals for people do and there is no bamboo Blue Cross.

If you want to experiment and learn how to fix them, there is one way to get some training in rod-craft techniques without risking your favorite rod. Go to a secondhand store and pick up a three-piece 9-foot junker such as an old rickety Wright & McGill, Montague or Heddon. Try to repair its old ferrules, reel seat or whatever. You also might throw away the butt section and make a two-piece 6-foot rod out of the midsection and top. I've known a number of handy people who built their small rods from the leftovers of 9-footers, and some of them are pretty nice. Many old, weepy, wet-fly-action rods make very adequate midge rods, able to handle No. 3 and No. 4 lines. Even if your repair job doesn't turn out to be a masterpiece, it will make an acceptable first rod for someone and give you the experience necessary to work on your own better ones.

One of the most important things to learn is how much heat to apply to your rod. Temperatures above 120 degrees can affect animal glues, and temperatures above 180 degrees can affect the composition of cane. Other rods, with natural glues, reach their critical temperature range between 150 and 200 degrees. It takes a feel to "understand" when to apply and remove heat from cane. Your junker rod can help you appreciate these subtleties.

Also, the "beater" rod you experiment with may not give you the confidence and skill necessary to repair your Leonard or Orvis, but it will, at the very least, teach you what the professional repairman is going through with your rod. You will be in a better position to think about the charges involved for repairing rods and whether they are justified or not.

Many of these repairs, such as handles and guides, are the same, basically, on glass and wood. With glass ferrules, however, it is often easier to simply replace the broken section than to monkey with it.

SET OR CAST

Sets are caused by the fibers becoming strained in one direction or the other, making the rod tip bend. Normally, bamboo recovers itself perfectly, but if the rod has been leaned against a wall for a long period of time, got too warm in a car or become strained playing a big fish, it can set. Paul Young always recommended turning his small rods around when playing a big fish, applying pressure on the other side. It might seem illogical, but you rarely see a Paul Young with a set in it.

The old-time remedy for a set is to hang the injured tip with a weight, like a reel, tied to the bottom for weeks or months. I have had very little success with this trick.

A more satisfactory way, though none are perfect, is to put it over a dry heat like a gas stove until it becomes so hot that you can barely touch it (it must be repeated that this is critical work), then straighten it out with your hands, sighting down the plane.

A folk cure for sets is to steam the bent section, but it is very untrustworthy. This treatment adds moisture to the cane, and that is exactly what you don't want. Good cane should be no more than 4 percent water, and steaming builds up the content. It does work, however, and some unscrupulous people use it to hustle rods.

If the set is really horrible, resembling a U-turn, the rod may have to be completely stripped down before the heat is applied.

LOOSE FERRULES

Ferrules become loose for two reasons. The simplest is when the connection between the male and female isn't snug—metal on metal, as it were. The other problem, more deeply seated, is when a ferrule isn't on the wood correctly.

You can repair simple metal-on-metal problems by taping the outside of the female and then tapping it very lightly against a piece of notched wood with a wooden mallet. This will slightly contract it. To contract a male, put it into a large drill bit chuck and slam the chuck quickly home by whirling the chuck key. This sudden pressure from the three points of the chuck will create swelling on three surface areas, creating an even, although temporary, pressure fit.

At best these cures are temporary. For permanent relief from nagging ferrule headaches, replace them with new ones. However, it's getting harder and harder to get the ferrules for hand-crafted rods. Leonard, Orvis, Winston and a few other custom makers might be enticed into parting with a few sets, but don't expect bargains. By the way, never try shape-changing tricks with the aluminum ferrules that were used on some lightweight rods during the 60's. The best thing to do is to get them replaced with good German silver ones.

If you have a problem with metal against wood, often manifested by a hairline or bigger crack in the ferrule terminal windings, you have a job on your hands. It is complicated because the better-quality rods had pinned ferrules. The quality makers drilled a minuscule hole at right angles through the ferrule and slipped a small piece of German silver wire through it. The quality of this drilling was so fine that on some rods it takes a magnifying glass and sensitive fingers to detect where the operation took place.

For starters, take a chance that the white lead used by rod

craftsmen to seat the ferrules has come loose. Unwrap the ferrule and place it over a flame. Heat it till your fingers can barely hold on and pray that the lead will settle in a stronger position.

If this scheme doesn't work, go back to finding the pin and knocking it out. Use a small jeweler's punch and try to drive the pin into a hole you have drilled in a small block of wood.

On some ultraquality rods, like Paynes, the ferrule won't normally heat off and has to be cut out. Payne, for one, heated his cane until the maximum contraction occurred, and then installed his ferrules. These ferrules get tighter and tighter with time, as the natural expansion and accretion of moisture occurs.

Being optimistic, let's assume you got the ferrule off with little or no damage to the rod. Clean the wood carefully with a dull knife and some cleaning solvent, like wood alcohol. Be extremely careful not to scrape any wood away.

Reseat the ferrule absolutely flat, using a heat-activated glue such as ferrule cement or arrowhead cement, or use the best all-around rod glue, Pliobond. Never, but never, use epoxy or any other heavy synthetic, or the ferrule will never come off again.

Line up the pin hole in the wood and metal, shove the ferrule on and replace the pin as best as possible.

If you can handle that, with these limited directions and no background, please don't hesitate to take a mail-order course in brain surgery.

DIRTY, GRIMY CORK, ETC.

If your handle is dirty but otherwise fine and you are a meticulous sort of person, it can be made spiffy again with household cleanser and small amounts of water. Don't overdo the water. Rinse it off with damp cotton cloth.

Gash, slash and chew marks from porcupines and other beatings require a decision—to replace or not to replace. If there is enough left to be comfortable and aesthetically pleasing after sanding, go that route. Slowly rub it down with a sandpaper that cuts the cork away without leaving ugly marks.

NEW HANDLE

Use a sharp knife or razor and split the old cork laterally until you are close to the wood or glass. Separate the cork and crack it off with your fingers. The reel seat doesn't have to come off unless it needs to be replaced if you take off the stripper and whatever other guides are on that section. Scrape the rod surface clean with a dull knife. When it's ready to go back together, slide on enough 1-inch cork rings to fill the entire length of the handle flush against the reel seat, making sure the rings are tight together. Remove the rings and lay them out in the same sequence. Cover the bottom 3 inches with Pliobond and shove the bottom ring against the reel seat. Spread some glue on the face of the ring, wiping all oozed glue off as necessary. Repeat this until you fill in the 3 glue-spread inches and repeat the process until the whole handle is replaced. Make sure the rings are tight against each other.

When you're finished, bind the rings with rubber bands to ensure that the pressure is equally distributed and leave it to dry like this overnight.

SHAPING A HANDLE

To keep the integrity of your original rod, you should have made an outline of the handle before breaking it off. The best way to recapture that shape or any other is on a wood lathe, no big problem since the stripper guide is already off. Use a fine file, then sandpaper as it turns down where you want it.

Without a lathe, you'll have to use a file to get it roughly where you want and then smooth it off with sandpaper held in your hand while turning the handle slowly around to imitate the lathe. This is a long process that's hard on your fingers.

CORROSION

Steel wool is best for removing corrosion, stains and whatever from ferrules and reel seats.

If the metal on your reel seat is dented, you'll have to remove it. This may require removing pins, alas, as well as the glue by heating. After you get it apart, buy a wooden dowel the same diameter as the inside of the seat and push or hammer it inside. This will help knock out the dents on seats and sliding bands on light rods as well.

Some of the better rods have anodized ferrules, and with time most of the coloring wears off. To restore the dark color, first remove all the old with steel wool and then clean the metal off with lighter fluid or white gas. Using a cotton swab, dab on a commercial brass blackener. Cold gun blues will sometimes work as well. It takes three or four applications. Between each one, rinse the metal off with cold water and allow it to dry. Eventually it will achieve the right satiny sheen. Varnish it afterward to give it some protection.

LOOSE OR WORN GUIDES

Check your guides over a few times each season. If they have ridges, bends or sharp edges, they can eat an expensive fly line in an afternoon. Remove faulty guides by cutting the silk along the foot, without scratching the wood or glass. Clean the area and file down the feet on the new guide so that it ascends as gradually in size as possible for smoother winds. Place it on the rod, tape one foot down and whip the other end on as neatly as possible. Remove the tape and wind the other side. To retain the exact color silk, use a color preservative (model airplane lacquer works well), and then spot varnish. You'll have to practice the wrapping process to get neat, tight and durable results.

MINOR FRACTURES

If a section begins to separate or develops a minor fracture, it will require a bind to fix. These splints are somewhat unsightly, but beauty isn't everything. Bindings are usually enough to restore a rod to practical duty. Use white silk for this job: for a minor repair use a very fine silk such as 6/0 and for a more major one, go up to a 2/0 or even an A.

Start the winding about ¼ inch below the problem area and continue wrapping tightly until the binding is ¼ inch above it. Whip the end off and then use spar varnish. Always use white thread because it will become transparent when the varnish is applied. Some very fancy rodmakers like Garrison used transparent windings.

In dire straits this technique can be used for even a complete crack. In such cases, when you have nothing to lose, take the two parts and try to reassemble the splits as best as possible. This is the one permissible time to use epoxy: on the inside of the break until it oozes out. Wipe off the excess, allow it to dry and wrap it with heavy thread. This will sometimes put life back into an otherwise worthless tip. I have a top for a Paul Young Midge that was thusly salvaged two years ago and it is still holding up.

TIP-TOP

If the top is grooved, bent or fractured, as most old agate tops are, heat it off. (Not too much heat, remember!) It will come off easily. Replace it with a good one, such as a Perfection, and stay away from the heavily chromed jobs. Melt a drop of stick ferrule cement onto the bamboo or glass and seat the tip-top, holding a match to it to keep the glue soft. Make sure it is aligned and wrap to its foot.

Al Troth's stone-fly nymph on snelled hook

VARNISH

There are two possible ways the varnish on your rod can go wrong, and both of them mean a lot of work. If your rod needs to be revarnished, you may as well go all the way and overhaul it completely, doing all the things in this chapter. It doesn't pay to do a halfway job. Back to basics.

If the varnish is brittle and cracked, lay the section flat on a table after removing the guides. Note which side the guides were on so that they can be replaced there. Also note the color, and the color combination of the windings. Begin scraping it carefully with a dull knife from the thickest part to the thinnest. Going the wrong way can mean a disaster for the rod. If the varnish has crystallized, it should almost explode off at the touch of a knife. Scrape it clean without scraping any wood away, and then finish the removal with a piece of steel wool wet with solvent.

If the varnish has become soft with time or has big sections missing, you should use a commercial paint remover. However, even if the directions call for water to remove the solvent, don't do it. Use white gas or alcohol instead. Allowing water to come in contact with your naked cane is asking for trouble over the long haul. Clean the cane off very carefully against a table or board with solvent and rub with steel wool until it is really smooth.

Now take the sections and hang them in as warm a place as you have around the house, such as near a furnace vent or wood stove if you are a cabin dweller like me. A couple weeks of this will sweat out moisture from the cane, a smart and safe practice.

Trick Time—At this juncture, a little-known trick is to boil some linseed oil to purify it and then rub it into the cane. This will penetrate all the stripped glue joints and cracks as well as any other possible opening. The oil will become as hard as the original glue if you allow it to set for a few more weeks.

When it comes time to varnish the cane, most people wrap on guides and whatever first. Perhaps a better way is to varnish first. This gives you a cleaner, smoother surface on which to put the hardware. A good cane rod should have at least three light coats. Each coat should be rubbed with a linseed-saturated cloth and a bit of pumice powder, giving the rod its smooth, satiny finish and also a good base for the guides. Whip the guides on in their original places and varnish them. Another minor trick is to use a bit of pumice powder after each coat on the wrappings. It smoothes them, giving the dazzling veneer of custom rods, but don't exert too much pressure or you'll weaken the winds.

This is just a basic starting point for rod craft. Books could be written about home rod care, but sadly aren't. The skills involved remain the possession of the artisans who do the building, and we amateurs must pay the piper or risk everything doing it ourselves. It's worth a try, but please don't practice on your best rod!

8

Rods for Power Fishing

I

To the tweed-encapsulated English angler, trout fishing is basically casting a fly to a nice-looking piece of water and hoping for
the best.

Of course these are generalizations or stereotypes, with holes
large enough to allow a mighty tarpon to pass. Nonetheless, a
case could be made that the British fish the fish and we fish the
water. Though American fly-fishing traditions are directly de-
scended from the English models, today they bear the same essential relationship as the martini-guzzling businessman does to his
dope-smoking son. What the majority of North American fly-fishermen practice is at least a modified form of water angling. Now of
course, this is not to say that we won't cast to a lunker trout rising
15 feet away. But that's not the general pattern of fishing day in
and day out.

Usually, casting to an individual fish would be a waste of time.
Our hatches are irregular on some waters and almost an insig-
nificant factor on otherwise excellent rivers. All too many of our
streams are beset by wildly fluctuating water levels, and there is
a terrible toll from a thousand and one forms of pollution. If you
get right down to it, on some of our best remaining rivers—most
of them, such as the Madison and Yellowstone, in the West—
emerging insects aren't that important to anglers flailing away
with Wooly Worms and Muddler Minnows. Those rivers do have
some wonderful hatches, like the huge salmon flies in early season,

but generally dry flies are not that productive. We Americans have to gather our troutfish where we may and not waste time putting our rods down and pouting because the fish won't rise to a hatching red quill.

In the fabled English limestone streams, which are akin to our spring creeks, hatches are a very regular occurrence, happening during the season on almost a daily basis. In this kind of water, with its even flow and temperature, insect larva form the bulk of a trout's diet. But in freestone waters, especially the larger ones, and in marginal trout habitats, fish are interested in a host of foods, ranging from minnows to mice and what other tasty morsels they can find. Like their semiferocious predator, *Americanus anglerus,* most of our trout would get awfully hungry if they had to depend on hatching insects for basic sustenance.

This isn't to say that there aren't important and wonderfully traditional hatches, especially in the East. They are the highlights of the entire fishing year for many people, but their centrality is itself an indictment of the poverty of much of our trout fishing— dependent as it is on a few spring hatches to make the year. In many places, stream-bed alterations cause the water temperature to rise too high for decent hatches to occur by mid-June or July, further limiting the dry-fly tradition. The semireligious fervor with which the March Browns, Cahills and Hendricksons are awaited is reminiscent of the Cargo Cults of the South Seas in which native practitioners build mock airfields to tempt back to their islands the long-departed U.S. planes that so greatly enriched their lives during World War II. Our cargo-cult anglers often search for the perfect dry fly to tempt back the long-departed fantastic hatches. Well, mystics are mystics, world wide.

Out of our relative lack of spectacular hatches, and the perpetual search for Moby Trout, has developed what can be called power fishing—the extreme outgrowth of fishing the water. Now, if we are going to operate on the premise that there are two kinds of inland trout fishing—the water or the fish—we have to understand this on a continuum rather than on an absolute basis. It isn't as if we were required to sign up in one school or the other before being allowed to fish. Most fishermen blend the two schools rather than specializing. Still, the two approaches to the sport are certainly distinguishable at the far ends of the spectrum.

The woman cautiously prowling the banks of LeTort Spring Creek clutching a Leonard Catskill probably thinks of herself as an ultralight tackle buff rather than an extreme historical example of fishing the fish. And on the opposite end of the scale, the angler heaving a 2/0 weighted spuddler across the Gallatin with a 6-ounce Orvis doesn't know he's the ultimate example of fishing the water. In this nation of extremes and faddishness, we have managed to take our tackle to the most drastic and actually excessive level. We have strayed a long way from our English forebears, whose taste in tackle has remained almost as constant as their protected trout streams during this modern era. Tactics and tackle have changed for us as the best fish habitats deteriorate—one keeping pace with the other in a sad race to nowhere.

In the nineteenth century, before most of the trout water in the East was brutalized, American fly-fishing buffs simply adopted English techniques, which were all that was available. This was before the dry fly revolutionized tackle in the late part of the century. The basic equipment had remained pretty much the same since the fifteenth-century days of Juliana Berners. Anglers used what we would call poles, but often very elegant ones. This primitive equipment worked quite well for our native brookies. Twelve-foot and longer rods and level, horsehair lines were used to heave two or more dazzling wet flies downstream. Early anglers could haul home a bushel basket of brookies with little technique and, alas, often did.

By the late nineteenth century, when the reclusive Theodore Gordon, our founding dry-fly father, began importing mooched floaters from his English counterpart, Frederick Halford, who systematized dry-fly angling, things had already taken a turn for the worse. A large proportion of the once cornucopic waters had become garbage dumps. Many anglers, including Gordon, were bemoaning the disappearance of our dumb but agreeable brookies, a fish as delicate as its ecosystem. With the same typical attitude we still have about environmental deterioration, we attempted to solve this problem without doing anything about the real cause— i.e., rampant profit-oriented technology.

The more arrogant brown trout, with an ability to tolerate waters of poorer quality, were imported from England and Germany and amply stocked. This newcomer, however, was not the kind of fish to swim idly by while a clown with a monstrous fishing pole stood a dozen feet away dragging a surrealist wet fly past its nose. The newly developed split-cane rod, with matching tapered silk line, was becoming generally employed by discriminating anglers, anxious to really fulfill, for the first time, the venerated seventeenth-century dictum of Charles Cotton, "Fish fine and far away."

At this point in history, we were still fairly close to our English fishing comrades, who had also picked up on the new floater gospel and its attendant equipment. But as the dry fly and its technique became more specialized for the new continent, the differences began to appear. The separation was well on its way by the time that George LaBranche penned his classic *Dry Fly and Fast Water* in 1914.

Our hackles had to be far stiffer than those necessary to float through the gentle English currents, and our success on those faster streams was increased by the water-resistant fly bodies that were constructed during this period. Our rods had to become shorter and tippier in response to choppy, drag-forming waters which required many short, drifting casts, rather than the long drifts of the chalk streams. The classic, gentle Eastern trout streams often proved the most ecologically fragile. It was the rougher, less accessible ones that managed to survive. So fundamental tackle alterations occurred in this country, and out of them came the tactic of fishing the water—fitted for streams with limited access, limited hatches and in some cases, unlimited anglers.

In many ways, tackle manufacturers have been oblivious to this development in fly-fishing, making it seem as if the major differences in rods are length and size. It is rarely made clear whether they are merchandising tackle designed primarily for short-distance casts or for tossing big flies a long way. This is a total difference, not just one of rod size or weight, and it's important for the critical angler. The classic approach to fishing the fish differs markedly in tackle requirements from the power-casting techniques of fishing the water. There are a few rods, like Leonard's LeTort series (no longer sold under that trade name) or Thomas and Thomas's Montana series, that are obviously designed for one particular function, but normally, catalogs leave you ignorant of the specific purpose of their masterpieces.

Admittedly, most anglers bridge the gap. Manufacturers are aware of this and capitalize on it with flowery, all-purpose descriptions, like "This rod handles dainty No. 20 dry flies in short casts but will also handle No. 2/0 muddlers for casts over 100 feet." Fishermen who haven't become hopelessly addicted to a limited form of angling and specific rod capabilities will use their favorite rod in a given size-and-weight category for the bulk of their endeavors. Nonetheless, it is the fisherman who adapts to the tackle rather than vice versa, and it can be tortuous to use dainty spring-creek tackle for casting big-bozo flies.

II

Like other contemporary tackle, power-fishing equipment came to the general public eye (though not in those terms) in the 1960's. Most important of the popularizers was Joe Brooks, who wrote many articles for the outdoor magazines on the use of big deerhair flies and exotic things like the blonde series, originally designed for saltwater use. For his excursions to the large rivers of Montana and other Western states, he favored rods of at least 8 feet that used lines of matching weight. His methodical casts of 60-plus feet, with unearthly feathery concoctions, were often rewarded with unearthly-sized trout. Of course, this whetted the reading public's appetite.

His outsized trouting weapons ran contrary to the wave of ultramidge rods that were in vogue during the late 50's and early 60's—popularized by anglers like Arnold Gingrich and Lee Wulff. But there was a catch in this ultralight business. If Gingrich's 6-foot, 3-inch, under-2-ounce Paul Young Midge could make a 10-inch rainbow feel like a 5-pounder, that was swell, but some people reasoned that it still seemed better to use that big rod and actually catch the 5-pounder. The little rod limits where its user can fish and how far he can reach out. These small rods still have many devotees and are the ideal tool for some situations, but perhaps they are best suited for the well-manicured private waters of the elite.

If it is possible to isolate a single source for the development of the power equipment, it would probably be the hairy, high-floating flies that began with the series that Lee Wulff designed in the late 1920's, bearing his name. These flies, popularized by Dan Bailey of Livingston, Montana, were originally designed by Wulff for the relatively new pursuit of dry-fly fishing for salmon. Then someone discovered that they were also winners for trout on the Western rivers. Out of the original hair-winged flies came monsters like the sofa pillows, other big trude flies and of course the muddler, which, with its multitude of offspring, is probably the Abraham of flies. It took a powerful rod to toss these curios the required distances into rough waters, and rods that mirrored those needs were first picked up by the small group of big-water freaks who were gathering around the major Montana rivers—especially around the Bailey shop on the Yellowstone.

The muddler and its family, in larger sizes from No. 6 onward, are best fished sinking—either weighted or with a wet shooting line—though they are often productive on top. Many of the traditional Eastern rods that formed the basis of our fly-fishing rigmarole shredded hopelessly after a season of King-Konging it. Anglers couldn't ignore the effectiveness of these deerhair beasties, so smart tackle makers went to work and came up with tools to do the job.

There was still another function for big flies and the power tackle necessary to deliver them. Fly users could work trout waters whose depth and force had made them off limits before and therefore the preserves of those archdemons, the spin fishermen. Also, as population pressures caused increased angling pressures, the angler who fished fat and far away had a decided advantage over his traditionalist kin. New horizons opened up in some of the biggest, roughest inland rivers and semideep lakes for those able to master the big tackle. Anglers such as Charlie Brooks, in his *Larger Trout for the Western Fly Fisherman* and *The Trout and the Stream*, groped with ways of systematizing this power fishing; gross as the fast-sinking lines and bulky, heavy flies may have appeared to those with refined sensibilities.

Another strain of power fishing was pilfered from the cultish West Coast steelheaders, who for decades created their own tackle, since manufacturers were often scornful of these peculiar people who spend winter days in chest-deep frigid water. Ingenuity has long been the key to success for steelheaders, who defend the use of strange tackle as being crucial to their sport. It's natural that they defend their mores, as it is a tradition that many of them were raised with.

The steelheaders' contribution to inland power fishing was the utilization of shooting heads and sinking lines. The windswept Western rivers are akin, ecologically, to the coastal rivers. In fact, I will admit to having to be told by companions, while fishing rivers in Washington and Oregon whether we were after native fish or wanderers from the seas, since the tackle and techniques were so similar. I'm a little smarter now, but fishing the big Montana rivers, especially in the fall when the browns are getting antsy, is simpler with light steelhead equipment. A shooting head, once you learn to handle it, is much easier to cast big flies with than a traditional double taper or even a weight forward. It's surely better to take gusty winds with a shooting head and a little help from the tricky but friendly double haul. Also, as everyone knows by now, river trout gobble nymphs or fodder fish much of the time and surface-feed comparatively little, so the quick-sinking lines favored by steelheaders are a real boon—though not always a pleasure to use unless the action is hot and heavy and you can overlook the difficulties.

One thing must be noted about this fishing—it's hell on tackle. Some of the real specialists of heavy-duty fishing, such as Dan Bailey's son, John, almost always use one line-weight heavier than rod manufacturers recommend. This makes casting easier under bad circumstances, but rods give up the ghost far sooner than under optimum conditions.

Red Monacle, another of the Livingston clique, once commented that my new Paul Young Para 15 was a fine rod, but that they didn't hold up well. After observing my nervousness over the soon-to-transpire demise of my find, John Bailey told me that Red had always used a line two weights heavier than the No. 5 Young recommended and he could cast halfway to everywhere for a whole season or more before cracking a tip.

Despite Joe Brooks and other early powerhouse anglers' predilections for 5- and 6-ounce Orvises that stretched to 10 feet at times, these monster bamboo rods have drifted out of favor, except for the dwindling few with strength to spare. Glass and, to a lesser but increasing extent, graphites have become, in the mid-1970's, the standard for this type of fishing. Even considering some custom-made exceptions like Peaks and Cumminses, glass rods normally don't inspire the dewy-eyed sentimental warmth of bamboo. If you smash glass, well, it's another $50 or so to replace it. If you crunch bamboo, it's the loss of a loved one.

Glass doesn't necessarily stand up to abuse better, but the angler does.

III

Given all that, how do you choose a rod for power fishing and, even more basically, how do you know if you need such a weapon in your arsenal?

You need such a specialized rod if you pass the following test:

1. Have you ever stood on the bank of a big river swooning in fear for your precious dry-fly rod after being handed a surefire fly which you suspected weighed more than the fish you were after?
2. Have you ever sat sobbing on the edge of a lake while four other guys were hooking monster fish with a huge spuddler, 30 feet farther than you could throw?
3. Do you find yourself lusting after the behemoths that are always in the middle of the river, 10 feet farther than you can presently wade and cast?
4. Would you want your daughter to use a shooting head?
5. Do you think bigger is often better?

If you answered any of the above questions affirmatively or realized that someday you might, then you're in the right chapter.

Though in a theoretical as well as practical sense, rod action is a subjective thing, there are particular things that are desirable in a long-distance pole besides the general qualities that make up good tackle. Feeling might be okay, but there are facts as well that should be observed before picking tackle.

Joe Brooks generally favored "slow action" rods, especially those impregnated ones sold by Orvis under that designation. The company went through a phase some time ago when their rods were merchandised as either fast, medium or slow action. Anyone who has followed the rodmaking technique at Orvis since they got back into the market heavily after World War II knows that the company favors powerful rods in all sizes.

Those slow rods are not like the soft-action rods that Leonard is famous for, but are closer to what contemporary anglers call parabolic rods. That means they bend all the way down. Now, without going into physics, it has always seemed to me that such a rod gives more control for long-distance casts. Its rhythms are such that the caster has time to correct errors, compensate for distances and get a good grasp of the variables in casts over 50 feet, where accuracy is an important factor. In some of the pocketed rivers, pinpoint control is required—the same sort of accuracy that has characterized dry-fly fishing from its inception. But dry-fly rods are never as forgiving when you make casting errors. Timing and rhythm are much more important with these tippy rods than with parabolics, where you can compensate in midcast.

It seems that more and more anglers are accepting the superiority of parabolic actions, or so-called parabolic actions, for this fishing. For me the ideal rod for power fishing as far as action goes is one of the Paul Young bamboo rods such as the Para 17, which takes an 8-weight line. But the problem is that this rod, like many of its wooden counterparts, is a beast to fish with all day. As I said earlier, anglers are increasingly using glass for these purposes. Manufacturers such as Winston and many others are now making slow, powerful rods.

To keep the line out of the water, handle big flies and cast long distances through winds, the rod should be at least 8 feet and closer to 9. Its line should be at least a No. 8, but keep in mind that heavy lines drag fearfully in river currents. In lakes, line weight isn't such a problem, and the question can be answered directly depending on distance, fly size and weight.

In essence, that is all there is to picking a rod for power fishing; make it a rugged and powerful one and bombs away.

9
Small Rods

I

There are many things about fly-fishing that lend themselves to miniaturization. Reaching angling puberty in the early 60's, when the mini craze was reaching its apex, I was swept up into its world, a world measured in grams and ounces.

I can remember the first time I saw an Orvis Superfine, the one-piece 6-footer that was the Maserati of rods in its heyday. I had seen other Orvises, but this was special. I was on Michigan's Au Sable River near Grayling, a college student up for the weekend, using my 8-foot plastic something-or-other that weighed a ton. Rounding a corner, I spied an angler who seemed the apotheosis of Western Civilization, bedecked in a fine vest, Hodgeman waders and that superb little rod equipped with a Hardy Featherweight. The dude cast his fly, a decent fish hit and the rod arched, as they say in the mags. Watching him skillfully land the fish accentuated my unworthiness and instantly made me resolve to re-equip myself, and since that day a dozen years ago, I have owned scads of small rods, ranging from 4-foot 4-inch to 6-foot 9-inch.

Short rods can be broken down into two general categories —the ultralights and the miniatures. This is another one of those fundamental differences glossed over by tackle manufacturers. What separates these two groups is not height, weight or action, but only the weight of the line each one takes. That wonderful

Orvis, weighing in at under 2 ounces, was not an ultralight rod by my current standards. It was a miniature trout rod.

Historically, small rods first got big-time publicity in the 1950's, but they have been around for a long time. In the 1920's, Hardy Brothers were boasting about their 7-foot CC DE France, coming in at 2½ ounces, as being the lightest practical rod possible. They also boasted how their champion caster had laid down some 80 feet of line at an exposition with the little brute. Of course they were hedging a little by talking about the lightest practical rod, but nonetheless that's where things were at. Perhaps they meant that with a smaller rod you couldn't control enough line, a thematic refrain of many such devotees of bigger sticks as Leonard Wright, author of *Fishing the Dry Fly as a Living Insect.*

Up until the 1950's most small rods used very light lines, like Leonard's famous 7-foot 39L, which took an IGI silk, or our No. 3. I suspect that even in those days these very light wands were most often used in private waters where wealthy management assured an abundance of trout. Fishing clubs have always been repositories for that kind of tackle experimentation; for example, by Arnold Gingrich, the small-tackle fanatic. Usually, anglers who hang around in public waters feel too much pressure to indulge themselves in restrictive luxuries.

In the 1950's the remaining fly-fishing coterie, a small number in comparison with the growing spin-fishing hordes, saw the rise of the miniature rod. Orvis really pioneered this type of tackle, though there are many claims for the honor. The notion was, as innovator Lee Wulff explained, a tiny rod that was sturdy and, equipped with a fair-capacity reel such as a Hardy Lightweight, was a match for anything up to salmon. It was supposed to be more fun, which has an element of truth but doesn't hold up to a finished analysis.

Wulff tested this thesis everywhere he could, including Scotland, where he engaged in an angling competition with Jock Scott. The contest was ludicrous in many respects, especially considering that neither of them caught anything in three days except for the lunatic salmon that hit Wulff's fly during a casting exhibition. At any rate, Scott used a traditional mammoth 15-foot English pole with lengthy roll casts and Wulff his tiny rod. The contest proved nothing, alas.

But the idea of using a rod that weighed less than 2 ounces rapidly caught on with many anglers, and those observed with anything longer than 7 feet were suspected of using chunks of sucker meat! By the late 60's, however, there were complaints about the miniature rods. They used lines that were relatively heavy for their size, depriving them of delicate action. Even a fine caster had to resort to the double haul to toss out line any distance with the stout miniatures, and it was difficult to control drag on the heavy, overweight lines.

Some of the rods sold during this period were ridiculous. One famous emporium on the West Coast recommended a No. 8 line for almost all of its small rods, including some tiny Winstons. This was a boon to the status-minded beginner, who miraculously found that he could quickly learn to cast his No. 8 line on the newly purchased and exorbitantly priced 6-foot bamboo rod. I would hate to see what one of those Winstons looked like after a couple of seasons of such abuse. Many people bought them because they were fashionable, not because they needed a special-purpose tool, and you could even find people fishing big Western rivers with these wonders, oblivious to their complete lack of suitability.

I know the things I have just said will ruffle some feathers because there are still anglers who love their miniature tackle. I wish them well with it—but hope they don't lead the innocent and naive unknowingly down this path. Despite the protestations of the Gingrich and Wulff set, the little rods really do have limitations. They are very awkward to cast in comparison with a longer rod and, though light and graceful in the hand, they have little of the grace of a larger rod when holding a line in the air. They must work too hard to carry a medium or heavy line.

On the other hand, I don't want to ignore the times when miniature rods come into their own. For instance, there is a small creek some 10 miles from my home near St. Ignatius. I fish this 25-foot stream quite a bit each season, especially along the lower end, where it empties into the mammoth Flathead River. The fish average only 10 to 12 inches, but at the mouth there is an occasional lunker cutthroat. As a compromise, I have settled on a 6½-foot Orvis DeLuxe as my rod for this water. After the runoff goes down in late June, most of the fishing is with dry flies, sizes 12 to 16. For this sort of "work" a delicate-action rod using a No. 4 or even a No. 3 line would be fine, since casts are rarely more than 25 feet and it is seldom windy. But about 25 percent of the time conditions call for the use of weighted nymphs and the muddler clan. On these occasions, a light-action rod is at a disadvantage, since big or weighted flies are hard to cast well on such rigs. Also, the stream mouth sometimes calls for throws as long as 50 feet when the cutthroat are cavorting in the rough, deep main river. I would feel outclassed with a truly light line.

Unlike Dick Eggert, who uses one of a brace of three-piece, 8-foot, No. 5-line Leonards, I think 4 ounces of wood is too much for small creeks. Dick is very much into the classic rhythms of the sport, extending classic rod actions into situations that I think somewhat inappropriate—either too light or too heavy. For me the choice here is between a larger rod, 7½ or 8 feet, that takes a No. 5 or No. 6, and a delicate rod that takes a No. 3 or No. 4. It can be resolved with one of the miniatures. There isn't any problem keeping 25 feet of line off the water with a small rod, and for longer casts, especially with a muddler, there isn't much necessity for this anyway.

I will be the first to admit that, in their place, the miniatures can be a lot of fun to use, especially impregnated or glass ones which can handle split shot or heave an extra 10 feet of line without worry. The danger is in the tendency to make them universals, applicable to every purpose in fly-fishing. Remember, the important thing in selecting tackle is to make wise compromises. Rarely will you find the fishing situation where all your gear is tailored to fit, unless you always fish the same water with the same technique.

II

The ultralight rods are very different from the miniatures. These rods take on the noble characteristics of their larger brethren and, for their very limited function, are a joy to behold and hold.

To me, this category includes rods only up to 6½ feet long and using lines no heavier than a No. 4. The archetypal model is the Leonard 36L or, as it is sometimes called, Baby Catskill. If you have ever seen or handled one, remember it is the standard by which all others should be judged.

Dick has a Baby Catskill in his collection, equipped with the minuscule Leonard Fairy reel. It takes a No. 2 level line, though Richard claims that it works better with a Cortland 444 running line, which is No. 1. At 6 feet, it contains the most ethereal ounce in rodmaking history, an ounce which waves dreamlike in the wind and gives the impression of being ready to snap at the first false cast. But it does cast, easily 20 feet, slow and gentle, and makes any small fish seem as glorious as the rod.

From my readings on the history of tackle, it seems that there have always been rods considered ultralights. Orvis made that boast about an 8-foot, 4-ouncer a hundred years ago. Hardy, Payne and the others continually made one rod or series of rods as their lightweights. By the 1930's, the 6-foot Maginot line was developed but not broached for a few decades.

In the mid 1960's, before fly-fishing tackle settled down to its current, somewhat stodgy seriousness of purpose, there was a lot of peculiar experimentation in rod length and action. Hardy, Payne and some other wooden makers put out 4-foot, 4-inch models, exalted as being pretty fair trout rods by people like Gingrich, who seems to believe at some level that smaller is better. Abercrombie & Fitch marketed a glass midget rod that used a special Gladding short-taper No. 5 line, and I used to take fiendish delight in casting it from the New York store's fishing department into the sleeping bags. Being a proper faddist, I had a tiny 5-foot rod made up for me by a relatively unknown Michigan maker and used it faithfully for two weeks before going back to longer rods, meaning 6 feet to me at the time. But despite Gingrich, all these rods I have seen, including the Paynes, were gimmicks at best and real stiffish dogs to cast all day, practically missing that quality we call action.

Orvis had a couple of rods under the 6-foot mark, and perhaps their Flea rod was the best of the tiny lot. In retrospect, however, it doesn't seem that anything resembling finesse can be achieved with either a bamboo or a glass rod that is too small. We have to face the reality that you can toss a line 30 to 40 feet with anything over 2 inches long, but it doesn't mean you're casting. To me casting means a certain balance between the rod and line and is relatively effortless. Some of the gimmicks are meant to throw a line in a style closer to spin fishing than fly-fishing.

True ultralight rods are available these days in all manner of actions from tippy dry-fly models to rich actions, like my favorite, the Paul Young Midge, considered by some anglers to be the modern paradigm for this type rod. At 6 feet 3 inches and under 2 ounces, the Midge can cast its No. 4 line as far as a sensible angler could care to place a fly with a small rod. It is truly a scaled-down version of a bigger rod, in this case the later Paul Youngs are the same in diminishing or ascending sizes, 7½-foot Perfectionist and the 8-foot Para 15. Actually, all of the later Paul Youngs are the same in diminishing or ascending sizes, one reason they have so many hard-core followers.

In general, it is hard to recommend an action for the light end of the rod spectrum. If you are consistent in your tastes, by all means get a small rod in that action grouping. If you are the whim type, follow your whim. Since pushing a small rod is silly (if you have to push it, either with fly size or distance, you should be using a bigger outfit), then get what pleases you. Almost all No. 4-line rods can handle flies as small as your vision will allow, so that isn't much of a factor either. If your casts are under 25 feet, you might consider a 6-footer or even smaller if there isn't much water where you will use it. For fishing streams and ponds that require longer casts, you'll have to go above 6 feet and maybe should consider a light rod instead of an ultralight.

Whether these rods are worth all the fuss is one of those almost entirely subjective matters, and I won't wet my feet. In Michigan I fished for two entire seasons with nothing but my Midge and had delightful times, from a tackle perspective and also because they were the first years of my commitment to trout fishing. What that might mean in 1975 is up to each angler, depending on where you fish, how you fish and why you fish.

10

Spring Creeks

Spending an afternoon on the bench overlooking Armstrong Spring Creek, south of Livingston, Montana, is a rewarding experience from a number of perspectives. With the wonderful Absaroka mountains over your shoulder and the broad rolling valley and gentle stream in front of you, it is a very relaxing place.

It's intriguing to watch anglers trying their skill on the myriad of fish that inhabit the creek. Despite a generally diminishing size from increased pressure, there are still hordes of free-rising trout—more per acre of water than in any other place in the state. Armstrong, handled for the past few years by Trout Unlimited and financed by some tackle manufacturers, has become one of the main testing and proving grounds for the new wave of fly anglers, even though it became in 1975 a pay-as-you-fish creek when the lease ran out. Like the Florida Keys, Henry's Fork of the Snake, the Madison and a few rivers with salmon, it is one of the paradigms of our sport, so for the most talented flycasters it is one of *the* places to go on the Western swing.

In some ways it is more fun for me to watch others on this mile-long, crystal-clear spring creek, with its steady flow of anglers, than it is to fish myself, as it's a bit crowded for my pure tastes. It is an ideal place to watch your fellow "piscators" perform and also a tackle freak's dream.

Despite an abundant sprinkling of journeyman glass rods held mostly by locals, the visiting anglers come decked out with their Sunday-best equipment. This is no roaring Madison, fraught with danger for the unwary, where one misstep can mean a crunched rod and chilling spills, but a gentle meadow stream, best fished with tiny flies. It is often a place of horrendous snobberies, where the hand holding a Payne goes thumbs down over the hand holding a mere Leonard and where you can get the social finger from a paw with a 2-ounce rod if yours weighs 3.

Still, although nearly everyone uses No. 16's and smaller, the tackle varies wildly. Spring-creek fishing has become very important to Americans recently, but the confusion over the proper tackle has yet to be straightened out.

The first book that I came across which mentions special tackle for these even-flow, even-temperature, highly vegetated waters is Vince Marinaro's *A Modern Dry-Fly Code*. This is a very important book on spring creeks, dealing mostly with the fishing around Carlisle, Pennsylvania, and the LeTort Spring Creek–Yellow Breeches axis. I was shocked to discover that Marinaro favored heavy lines and long leaders for use with the tiny dries and terrestrials he helped innovate with Charlie Fox. He talks about experimenting with an AA taper, our No. 9 line, to help straighten out his leader—a perennial problem in this kind of fishing.

As techniques for spring-creek fishing drifted far from Marinaro's 1950's solutions, they, like most other fly casting, entered an ultralight phase. By the 1960's you needed nothing more than a 6-foot, 1½-ounce rod to fish the No. 18's and No. 20's right on such streams from East to West. You would see half-submerged anglers waving things that looked suspiciously like toothpicks. They were fun to cast and play a fish with, but were certainly not the answer. Nonetheless, we true believers struggled vainly with them.

Today, perhaps 50 percent of the spring-creek anglers still remain faithful to rods under 7 feet, but they have decided disadvantages. As Leonard Wright so well explained in his *Fishing the Dry Fly as a Living Insect*, small rods mean quick drag. A short rod just doesn't keep enough line off the water for a long enough time. It seems to me that leader drag and pull is also a more critical problem with the small traditional and no-hackle flies that are tied for spring creeks. Wright was describing caddis-fly angling on Eastern freestone streams, but the problems with the little rods are equally true on spring creeks with mayflies and nymphs. He favors ultralong rods, over 9 feet, with light lines—a combination that I find boring to use after a short time.

To me the compromise rod for this situation is a light 8- or 8½-footer that takes a No. 5 or No. 6 line and is able to cast it

50 feet, if you happen to see a lunker rising at that distance. It doesn't matter if the rod is bamboo or glass, as long as its tip is soft enough to handle 6X and 7X leaders and matching flies. Graphites don't mix too well with these fine leaders. Some of the rods currently being passed off as spring-creekers are a bit too soft for the purpose and not able to bridge the gap between handling a light leader gently and turning it over. Straight leaders and good control are important when you are fishing where you are often required to lay your fly gently on a particular fish's nose.

In this type of fishing, tackle is very important, especially for the beginner. Anglers like Dick Eggert, who are masters of the light line and weepy rod, can handle even strong winds with such equipment, but you can't hope to achieve that if you're just starting out. It's hard to find a good rod that takes a No. 4 line and is long enough for spring creeks. Such a rod, however, would be ideal. Most of the 8-footers that take really light lines are too soft for the moderate-range casting that is sometimes required. Here again, there has to be a compromise. Settle for a little heavier line. You can easily compensate for the extra grams of a one-weight-heavier line with an extra foot of leader length.

I am a firm believer that experience can negate the need for fine tackle, if you choose to go that way. My Post Creek neighbor, Dave Harriman, uses short, level leaders, nonplussed flies and downstream distance casts. On mutual trips, he will do at least as well as Dick or I with our fancy equipment and respective traditional and hypermodern techniques. But Dave, who raises trout for a living, is a true expert in their behavior and idiosyncrasies. He successfully replaces technological advantages with knowledge of his quarry. However, it takes years to develop such talents, and the rookie spring-creeker is foolish to think otherwise. On the other hand, success won't come instantly with fine tackle either, as the hordes of anglers who look as if they have stepped directly from the pages of an Orvis or Leonard catalog are proof. These people, who often fish only a few times a year, seem to believe they can buy their way into competency—a foolish error, as their strafing casts attest. Get equipped for spring creeks, if it intrigues you, but don't think there are any real shortcuts to their intricacies. You may learn to cast in an hour, but it takes much practice to learn delicate accuracy.

11

Warm Waters

Outdoor writers usually get tears in their eyes when they speak of panfish. Like apple pie, good ole Mom and the flag, these spiny-finned fish are a sentimental subject. And like those other things, they are deserted at the first opportunity to seek trout, tunny or tarpon.

Let's face it. You would have to be pretty snooty to choose not to fish at all if panfish and their kin were the only things within casting distance. On the other hand, I have yet to meet the fly angler, though they undoubtedly exist, who would choose warm-water inhabitants over native trout in a clear, cold stream. There is more excitement, challenge and tradition in trout fishing, little doubt about it. As one raised in the tidewater area, who learned fishing on nonsalmonoids, I can confidently say this. Ernie Schwiebert once responded in all seriousness to my suggestion that we go bass bugging for a break from trouting that he used to like the sport, but felt that it hurt his reflexes for salmon and trout fishing.

At times, though, living in what's left of Montana's trout para-dise, I get strange twitchings—especially in March, when I think of the yellow perch running in Maryland rivers. I learned late to fish for those tasty beasties with a fly, after spending years seeking them with a—yes—spinning outfit. My angling "biorhythm" is still set for early spring when the perch get itchy. I then suffer a few months before things even start to thaw in my current mountain home.

One day, when a six-year-old inner-city Baltimore kid, I was browsing through the library and came upon some kind of boy's guide to fishing. I had some trouble reading a book for twelve-year-olds; however, in one chapter I haltingly made out that flies were an excellent bait for panfish. I rushed home and, using stealth and a jar, snared some houseflies. The next day at the golf course I had a miserable time trying to impale them on those damned kirby hooks. After that one awful experience, I gave up on fly-fishing for about six years.

Then, during one of those ballyhooed East Coast George Washington's birthday sales, I got a fly outfit. I will never forget how rotten it was. The rig consisted of a three-piece, 9-foot Wright & McGill bottom-of-the-line bamboo rod, about a No. 1 silk or linen level line and a rickety frame reel made in Japan. Not bad for a buck, maybe, but it was terrible. Casting more than a rod's length was impossible, and I never managed to take one sunny with it. I gave up and went back into spinning in a week. For six more years I avoided fly-fishing.

In my next fling with the sport, a wonderful shopkeeper in Towson, Maryland, refused to take any of my Marine Corps salary unless I purchased a balanced outfit and, most especially, a double-tapered line. I did and it worked. After that I spent a few years bouncing around the Southern states, especially Maryland, with that ten-dollar, 7-foot Angler rod, a Scientific Angler No. 6 line and of Pflueger Medalist reel. It was an all-right outfit and cured much of my fly-fishing pessimism. Before this, I was convinced that you needed superhuman coordination to cast a fly.

This is still a pretty good basic rig for panfish, though too light for bass and pickerel. I think that most of this fishing, usually done in ponds and small lakes, with small cork bugs (preferable to hair dry flies, it seems) and requiring short (20- to 30-foot) casts, is best done with a weight-forward line. There isn't much need for elaborate false casting, so a double taper is excessive, especially since you will sometimes want to use a big fly (No. 4 and larger). It takes a variety of flies to entice the spectrum of fish, from bass to crappies through bluegills and pickerel. In the 1975 *Sports Afield* fly-fishing issue, some famous outdoor writer once again recommends using a level line for this action, but don't do it. The functionality of level lines is one of the recurring myths of the sport, and it's nonsense. A cheaper tapered line is better for everything, except hanging clothes, than an expensive level line.

I think you can also get away with a shorter rod, especially since some of this fishing is done from a boat or in places that

Martin automatic reel on three-piece, 9-foot Heddon rod, panfish rig

don't require a high back cast. If you are only trying for small
fish, you can manage with really light stuff, if you're that way.
System 4's from Scientific and some other light rods are fine for
bluegills, just-under-the-surface crappies and small bass, when
weeds aren't a problem. This is also a fine area to use some of
the so-called ultralight rods that are around 6 feet and take a
No. 6 line.

The general rules of thumb in the "Basics of Rod Buying"
chapter hold here, taking into consideration cast length, fly size,
water conditions and fish proportions. One other thing to consider
is the length of leader you will be turning over. I like a long one
(9 feet) for all surface fishing, even with small bugs, so I need
the power to lay it out semistraight. Some people like really short
leaders (down to 5 feet) but I prefer the security of a leader
that doesn't insist on casts being absolutely consistent and delicate. A small reel will do the job well because there is no need
for a lot of backing, and automatics will be fine if you fish from
a boat. A sink-tip line is sometimes beneficial, especially during
late summer when the fish are seeking cooler waters. The nicest
thing about fly-fishing for the warmwater breeds is its simplicity.
A few small surface poppers, a few sinking nymphs, maybe some
streamers and that's it. None of the rigmarole of trout fishing,
which can be both beauty and curse.

As you move up the scale into bass equipment you need
stouter gear. It's always hard to generalize about equipment for
fly-fishing, as circumstances determine what you'll need. In my
last foray into Florida, I took an old Orvis Shooting Star and a
System 8. They worked okay for shell crackers, baby tarpon and
some other peculiar Southern fish, but I had to borrow stuff for
big-time bass bugging in Lake Jackson. Both my outfits were just
too light; the No. 8 lines couldn't handle the monster 2/0 bugs that
seemed right. Disliking sloppy, "forced" casting, I borrowed a
System 10, which fixed that problem at least.

One unofficial guide, a connoisseur of the huge live minnow and garish rubber worm, took me on an angling tour of some Tallahassee-area lakes, where 15-pound bass had been coming out with shocking regularity. He remarked that he had never known that bass could be taken on flies. He still doesn't, actually. I was skunked five different ways!

I've found that, unless I'm fishing in really open water, the usual recommendation of having 50 yards or so of backing is meaningless, except maybe as psychological booster. Of all the places I've fished for bass, 99 99/100 had so many snags that, if I didn't haul the fish out immediately, it was gone. Of course having backing on a reel to fill it up is always smart. It is quicker to retrieve that way, but its other function isn't very useful.

You can tolerate a bigger rod, relatively, for bigger warmwater fish than for trout, simply because you don't cast as much. This type of angling is a much more measured affair, with each cast in a lake or pond at rest much longer. Just remember that it is very frustrating to be unable to cast a big fly or bug on too light an outfit or to be unable to handle a good-sized fish in weedy water. It's worth going up a line size or two just to be sure.

Turn-of-the-century snelled dry fly for trout and bass

The same holds for fishing brackish water along the coasts. Though it may resemble inland fishing, you run into some big fish occasionally and at times want to get down pretty deep. You have to compromise somewhere. For much of the hickory shad fishing along Maryland rivers like Deep Creek, I got along with my trouting stuff, but when the white shad came around I was outclassed. The hickories, averaging a pound or so, can be fished in medium-sized streams, which can be waded almost everywhere, and a sink-tip line gets you down easily. The constant angling chum of my Maryland youth, Peter Grafton Streett, used a 9-foot, bass-bugging bamboo Montague Redwing for even hickories, but he was always a person of extremes. When I faced the raging Susquehanna or even the smaller Delaware or Connecticut with my puny 7½-footer, it was useless to even try, except on the rare occasions when the shad would rise. The white or American shad like the bigger waters for spawning, and it takes big tackle to get the shad flies down to their haunts.

Along the West Coast, where the white shad was introduced, many anglers consider them junk fish, mainly because of the heavy tackle required to entice them. Those anglers have never had a breakfast of shad roe and scrambled eggs, or they would consider a derrick and hoist worth their while to get the shad on the plate!

Those who fly-fish for shad mostly use their steelhead equipment because of the long casts, heavy waters and depths involved. It's a shame, among hundreds of shames in our treatment of the environment, that these great-fighting and great-tasting fish can no longer spawn in small rivers and streams because pollution has ruined the runs. For their size, they could put up battles to match the best of the salmon and steelhead, adding a great new dimension to American angling.

Some people have always argued that for pickerel and their big cousins, the northern pike, stout equipment is necessary. Despite their toothiness, I don't believe it requires anything other than our general rules of rod considerations. A small wire leader can negate the most ferocious jaws. The big streamers, Mylar and marabou combinations, that these very predacious fish like best are the biggest factor in deciding on tackle size. In Canada, where northern pike fishing is a big pastime, it sometimes requires heavy-sinking stuff to find them. Here again, water conditions and fly size determine things, not teeth. You may go for these streamlined fighters in water that is heavily vegetated, another important consideration.

It is a good idea to take out a general-action rod rather than one which will balance only with a particular line. A rod that takes a No. 5 line for long casts and a No. 6 for average lengths is desirable in warmwater angling. If need be, a rod of this type can be overloaded with a No. 7 line when you have to use big bugs or streamers. There are some good rods with these capabilities, especially the graphites, which can sometimes take anything from a No. 6 through No. 8 handily. You won't generally run into this sort of variety when doing other fly-fishing, but for the warmwater breeds, tackle versatility is a good idea.

12

Salmon, Steelheads and Saltwater Fishing

I

There are big rods and then there are BIG rods, and their function is to catch big fish.

In a nutshell, that is the philosophy of many of the most seasoned anglers I know. I first heard it from veteran West Coast steelhead-and-salmon catcher Russ Chatham, who, now that he lives south of Livingston, has begrudgingly become a trout fisherman.

One day a few years ago, when we had just met and were sort of feeling each other out, he stared at the 9-foot Paul Young Florida Special I used for big Montana waters and shook his head. It was a beautiful rod, though after an hour its 6 ounces took a terrible toll from even my 6-foot 3-inch 200-pound frame. Russ is of the big-water steelhead school that fishes continuously from sunup to sundown, biting hunks from a sandwich between false casts; but taking this rod to the Yellowstone was too much for even his sensibilities.

"You know," he said, "A trout is a twelve-inch fish."

"What?"

"That's right. You can catch a big one now and then, but most trout are twelve inches or so, no matter where you fish in this country. To act like they are saltwater or anadromous creatures is really dumb."

I had never thought of it, but in an important sense he was right. Many of the stay-at-home Montanans I'd fished with over the past few years had fooled me with their tackle. Size is relative, of course, and our search for bigger and bigger trout had blinded me to their place in the sun. I still occasionally use sinking lines, shooting heads and such paraphernalia, but more understandingly now. If I ever get into the mood for monsters, I head for Florida or the West Coast and don't waste my time on Montana rivers.

Now, for most of my fishing around home, I use nothing over 8 feet, because almost everything I catch is going to be around 12 inches. I know this runs contrary to the teachings of such head-hunters as West Yellowstone's Charles E. Brooks, author of *Larger Trout for the Western Fly Fisherman,* who fishes for trout as if they were steelhead or tarpon. These days I believe that trout fishing should be done as gently as possible, like love. I wish Brooks and his kindred souls all the luck in the world catching trout over 5 pounds, but there is a limit to how much I'll compromise for those rare encounters.

I've taken this roundabout way of getting into the hefty-tackle category to clear up the difference between it and the heavy fresh-water stuff used by some people who specialize in catching the biggest trout they can. The big-league tackle runs the gamut between the still-delicate, modified-trout-type equipment used for the noble but disappearing Atlantic salmon to the clubs that are used for subduing tarpon running over a hundred pounds. Somewhere between the two is steelhead gear. My experience in this fishing is firmly admitted to be somewhat limited, but there has been some direct contact between me and such beasties. There has also been a great deal of conversation between me and some fine practitioners of these pursuits. Besides, when has a lack of knowledge ever stopped a writer from expounding on a subject?

Salmon fishing probably includes the greatest range of tackle of any part of fly-fishing. It ranges from the ephemeral, ultralight stuff used by such equipment brahmins as Arnold Gingrich and Lee Wulff on Canada's east-coast rivers to the 12- to 16-footers still favored on the big waters of the British Isles and Scandinavia. There is just no way in the world that I'm going to get into the midst of an argument over rod length with salmon fanatics. I'd just as soon argue about socialism with a John Bircher. Not only could I never win, but I could easily get injured.

Nevertheless, as in any area of tackle choice, there are some basic considerations for those going at least half-ass objectively into buying equipment. Here again, the deciding factors should be

(left) Dark Gordon steelhead fly

(right) Low-water Atlantic salmon fly

the size of the fly that is going to be used, the length of the cast, the current of the rivers and where your fly should go in them, your physical size, and, maybe, the size of the fish. Before the dry fly entered the salmon-fishing picture in the first few decades of this century, the tackle picture was clearer. There were some daring heretics who favored rods as short as 10 feet, but for most of the business, a dozen feet or more was the generally accepted size.

However, mostly under the directorship of Wulff, who popularized the deerhair flies bearing his name, there was a rapid change of fashion toward light rods for fishing medium-sized dries or nymphs near the surface. The traditionalists ignored this North American tomfoolery, going their European way. Like the Russians and Americans searching for a detente, these two groups of salmon fishermen have recently been heading toward a common ground of equipment. It has probably been reached in the area of No. 8 tackle, now recommended for general light-salmon equipment by all but the holdouts. This is the same general equipment used for big-river trouting, but there are some significant differences, mostly because of the big dries, which play a very minor part in power trout fishing but are used for salmon whenever possible.

A salmon-fishing trip is a big expense, and if money matters to you, find out what the acceptable norm is where you are going. This doesn't mean that you should obediently accept the dictates of the region. Some of the blindest people on the subject of tackle I ever met have been "locals." It seems that the more isolated the geographic area, the more limited the knowledge folks have about what you can use to catch fish.

(left above) Saltwater streamer

(right top) Plastic hand-painted popper for strip bass in brackish water

(right center) Deerhair popper for bass

(right bottom) Deerhair moth

I was once told by a professor of language that when a group of people settles an area, like the Italians in parts of New York, the English on North Carolina's Outer Banks and the French in Quebec, their language develops into its own dialect, distinct from the mother tongue. This also seems to happen with tackle. When a group of people make their first contact with fly-fishing, they pick up the techniques of the originator and develop it from there, often erratically along its own course. I've found myself in Montana backwaters where it still is believed that "their" trout won't hit dries and that only a 9-foot rod can handle "their" water. In microcosm, it's like the transoceanic debate over rod length. Anyway, local customs can be a guideline or starting point for your salmon tackle choices and from there you can apply some logic.

There is one other major consideration in salmon tackle affecting, at least for me, the choice of equipment—tradition. That is a word I've purposely tried to avoid using, but now I have no choice. It can become a mystical concept and also be used as a put-down against anyone not following your dictates. More than once I've been sneered at by the "illustrious" for using gear that was just "unacceptable." It is for this reason that I hate to—excuse the choice of phrases—open that can of worms, but when it's all that will describe the phenomena I have no choice.

Some of the loveliest rods and reels I've ever seen were created for salmon fishing—long Paynes and Leonards, graceful Thomases and imposing Hardys, equipped with Vom Hofes, Walkers and Bogdans. The upper echelons of tackle spiritualism. Despite the elitism, snobbery and social obliviousness so often a big part of this rarefied atmosphere, I love it, hopefully checking its negative aspects and emphasizing the craftsmanship and care lavished upon it.

Let's face it, fly-fishing for salmon still ain't a sport for the "common man," and whenever one of us plain folk gets an opportunity to engage in it, there's a lot of luck and good manners involved. Sure, there are still a few places where a relatively limited amount of money (relative to a new car) can get you a fair, if not decent, place to try it out, but that isn't a regular experience. You usually have to have money or acquire friends who do—both consuming endeavors that take time away from regular fishing. Of course you have the option to fantasize about an archduke or the like seeing your graceful casts on a home river and inviting you to accompany him to his beat on the Alta in Norway for July. You can also believe in the tooth fairy.

So if, by hook or by crook, you have the opportunity to partake, maybe you should go all the way—a fine bamboo rod and all the fittings, including some delectable nineteenth-century-type wet flies, so much snazzier than the plebeian hair flies developed in North America. Those elegant three-piece, 9-foot-plus rods are still very usable for salmon angling and can often be bought for a third less than a trout rod by the same maker. You may not get to use it much, but it could be one of those prized mementoes on which memories of a lifetime are constructed.

"Hi, Bert. Have you seen my ten-foot Payne salmon rod? Takes a Number eight line . . . just perfect for my trip to the Miramachi!" Ah, sweet delicacies!

Enough said.

II

Capitalists are to workers what salmon fishing is to . . . ?

Give up? Steelheading, of course. It is the antithesis of glamour. Picture the Atlantic salmon angler standing upon a green bank, gillie at hand with lunch and whatever. His wife, the Duchess of Deuteronomy, attired in similar tweeds, stands at his side with a slightly smaller bamboo rod. The poor but happy peasants watch their lord and lady seek the gorgeous salmon, a fish wise enough to know its place—at the end of milord's line.

Now, let's go to the West Coast, where three guys are up to their assets in water that's too cold to freeze. They've been double-hauling lead-core lines for three hours as truck drivers shout obscenities at them from the bridge 300 years downstream.

Got the picture? Steelhead fishing has been dubbed "democracy's answer to the Atlantic salmon," by Dr. Marshall Bloom of Hamilton, Montana. It's an apt description. Steelheading takes place under rough, if not actually dangerous, circumstances, and for someone not smitten by the bug, it can be like the hardest type of work. Except for the remote fly-in rivers along the coast of western Canada, it is done in places accessible to almost everyone in the right areas with a car. The sport has become more and more popular for dedicated anglers unwilling or unable to make the sacrifices necessary to seek the Atlantic salmon.

Despite the many dilettantes who try their hand at it, the hard core with their specialized gear take the highest toll of these sea-run rainbows. The tackle used by specialists like Russ Chatham, Bill Schatt and their crew is, by most standards, the crudest in all fly-fishing. Russ's favorite rods for these seafaring monsters are made in a matter of minutes from almost any hefty glass blank costing a couple of bucks; tape on the guides and the reel and that's about it. Enough to turn a self-respecting trout fisherman's stomach.

But these people don't fool around. Russ once showed me a System 10 Scientific Angler rod that I thought would be perfect for his fishing. Nope, even good rods like that last only a matter of days before shredding under the tasks assigned to them. These guys aren't normal steelheaders but the supermen of the sport, and they use whatever it takes to catch the fish. That will often include lead-core lines that weigh literally hundreds of grains. They fish every minute of daylight, and it takes a horrendous toll on the tackle.

On the other hand, there are a number of steelheaders not so manic about the sport who use fine bamboo rods—mostly Powells and Winstons—or custom glass rods like Peaks. They are very happy with their tackle and would never consider imitating the crudities of Chatham. You have to be honest with yourself. Do you really fish hard? If so, how hard? Are you a tackle destroyer? Is your rod worth more to you than a fish? Those are the questions you'll have to answer.

You don't have to use brute equipment if you fish within 75 feet and fairly close to the surface. But torrential rivers requiring monumental distances are another matter. Lead-core stuff, it can't be overemphasized, is murder on rods, and there are conditions where it is the only thing that will catch the fish. By the way, some of the more dainty anglers around look down their upturned noses at lead-core heads and the like, believing them closer in theory to spinning or, even worse, trolling. At an earlier time I might have agreed, but after watching Russ and others perform with such equipment, I'm convinced that in the right hands it has the same rhythm and, excuse me, poetry that the rest of fly casting has. Russ, who is the best practical caster I have ever met, can handle a metal-centered head the same way Dick Eggert handles a No. 3 double-tapered line. One big difference is the importance of never making serious casting errors with the superheavy lines—

it can't be argued that getting beaned with the No. 3 is anything like getting K.O.'d with a 450-grain lead core.

Here again we get to that point where the basic considerations in choosing tackle come to the fore, with one minor difference. Many of the top steelheaders prefer an even-action or semiparabolic rod, believing that it handles long casts with sinking lines best. Tippy rods generally aren't up to the task except for relatively close-in dry-fly steelheading, a very minor part of the game. But on some rivers you shouldn't go out with just one steelhead rod unless you are close to home or camp where reinforcements wait. Even under the best conditions you have to do plenty of casting; loose ferrules quickly disappear and a weak spot on a two-piece rod can make it a three-piecer.

When you get right down to it, modern steelheading is one area where the rod isn't as significant as it is in most others. Here's a place to skimp a bit in dressings and fittings, so you can get that snazzy trout rod for use in tamer waters. Once again, my own opinion and taste will probably run contrary to the opinions and tastes of many experienced steelheaders.

I never accept collect phone calls!

III

Recommending tackle for the oceans and flats is a tricky business. Conditions vary greatly, as can be easily imagined. On some days on the Florida Keys, the target will be bonefish around 10 pounds, and the next day or even same afternoon, the quarry may be the huge tarpon. But the common characteristics are almost invariably long casts and a driving wind, coupled with big flies or bugs.

All of the saltwater species that will come to a fly, from barracuda to marlin, like their food big and usually fast-moving. In what Karl Marx would have called another example of the unity of opposites, much saltwater fly-fishing is closer to English chalk-stream angling than anything else. You are casting to individual fish, which requires pinpoint accuracy. A few inches either way from a given fish's nose can mean the difference between success and failure. The casting is not the regular business that most of us are accustomed to, as you don't begin letting out line till you see what you want, and then it has to be done quickly and well. Fishing the water is pretty meaningless in something as

Fin-Nor No. 3 reel on heavy saltwater rod with fighting butt

big as an ocean. So you can get away with a rod that is stouter than any you would use for all-day casting, since a few dozen casts will usually suffice for a very successful outing.

Another factor to remember is that the line will cause a terrible shadow that can easily scare fish in shallow water. Double-hauling, though very overrated in most angling, is a lifesaver on the flats, where all you want is 30 feet of line and a shoot to get your fly 60 feet away. One false cast and then let it go. The hundred-footers raved about by Lefty Kreh and other aficionados are rarely needed. If you can have pinpoint accuracy with 60 feet of line, you have most of it beaten.

Don't forget the almost constant wind. It really helps to have a line heavy enough to drive through it. It's one thing to try out your techniques alongside a shop or from a casting platform and another to have to buck an ocean breeze.

Most of my serious flats-fishing friends, like Guy Valdene and Tom McGuane, keep a System 8 outfit on their flatboats for tiny close-in stuff, but start getting serious with No. 10's and range up to clothesline diameter No. 12's. Though their trout tackle is impeccable, with the corrosive powers of the salt water and the brute force of the fish, good glass is where it's at. Or, perhaps, graphite. There really isn't much reason to use bamboo in the ocean. Despite impregnation, it still is threatened by the nature of the brine and too expensive to risk such beatings, as well as being unnecessarily heavy.

This is another expensive kind of fishing to do right—complete with guides, boats and whatevers. Check out local conditions. Retrograde idiosyncrasies about equipment have not had much of a chance to blossom in the salt as yet, and the regional advice you get will probably be solid. Though people have been fly-fishing Florida's coast since at least the turn of the century, it has only recently become systematized to any real degree. Tackle manufacturers, most anxious to spread the sport to this new frontier, have people testing equipment, so you can drop them a line for specific questions on what to use where.

Just go as light as you can get away with, but don't take chances on the mysterious powers of these fish. Also be sure to wash off your tackle each day in fresh water to avoid the horrendous encrustations that quickly accumulate.

13

Specialized Rods

As the dope addict in the Grade B movie always says, "I ain't hooked. I can take it or leave it." Well, it's with that sort of trepidation that this chapter is offered. Once you start to descend into the tackle morass, it's hard to emerge unscathed. You can wind up with a rod for every river you fish, then every pool, then one for the top end of the pool and one for the bottom and so on and on and on. . . . Let me begin with a strong disclaimer. There is no sound reason why your basic rods cannot fulfill any of the following tasks. Amen.

BACKPACKING AND TRAVELING

Not very long ago there would have been little reason to delve into rods specially made for hauling around. Most rods were constructed in three pieces, and a three-section 8-footer is easy enough to take with you anywhere. But then, as rods got smaller and lightness became a fetish, the two-piece fashion took over except for some hard-core holdouts like Dick Eggert, who wouldn't own a two-piecer over 7 feet for reasons of convenience. Looking back at tackle literature, you can chart the movement for the two-piece supremacy by the spate of what could be dubbed "antiferrule" articles. Paul Young decried ferrules as a necessary evil, and he made only two-piece rods. Other rodmakers and fishing writers supported his arguments, and the three-section stick began a decline.

I think that the automobile had at least as much to do with the popularity of the two-piece rod as ferrule considerations. The access to individual transportation that the auto provided the public after World War II made the length of the rod case irrelevant. It became treasonous not to have your own car, and as we became shamefully dependent on the wasteful roadway system that scars this country, mass transportation was sadly neglected. We now have lines of vehicles with one occupant apiece, heading for waterways destroyed by roads and other technologies necessary for the automobile. But that's another story.

Anyway, as those who have done a lot of traveling with tackle know, the car is okay for two-piece rods, but handling a 4-foot rod case on a bus, train or plane can be a hassle. Of course, there has always been some sort of rod especially designed for portability. In the fifteenth century, Dame Juliana Berners described in her *Treatyse of Fysshynge Wyth an Angle* how to make a walking-stick rod. In the last hundred years, there have been scads of rods described variously as train rods, boat rods, bike rods, poacher's rods and the like.

Some of the better ones were described as steamer rods and were made by outfits like Leonard for a very long time. They were broken down into five, six, seven and so on small pieces and would fit in traveling luggage. Some of these were top-quality products, but their actions were often poor because of the abundance of ferrules. I have such a marvel. It is 7 feet long and breaks into seven sections, each one with a clunky brass ferrule. It is at least forty years old and has one of the worst actions imaginable. In the 1930's, some companies started making such portable rods and calling them "pack rods."

Their real distinction came during the 60's, when backcountry angling was becoming popular and most rods were two-piece. Companies like Wright & McGill and Fenwick, riding the crest of their glass-ferrule revolution, began to market pack rods. The early ones were as terrible as all the other early glass rods. The makers were too amazed that anyone could actually build a rod from fiberglass to be concerned about such incidentals as action or design. Those hiking far into the mountains weren't very concerned about such things either.

For the pack-angling specialist looking for a nice rod, there was a four-piecer made by Leonard and the well-known Orvis Rocky Mountain, which was a three-piece 6½-footer taking a No. 6 line. Today there are many models to choose from, and this is another area where glass far outshines bamboo.

The general considerations for a pack rod are the same as with any other rod choice, with the addition of convenience. A decade ago you usually had to sacrifice quality for ease of carrying, but no more. From the nicely engineered new Fenwicks to the custom-made models, glass ferrules and general synthetic-rod technology have made it possible for some pack rods to be good enough for all-around use. Just about every maker now has at least one rod described as being for traveling. It will usually be in four sections, but sometimes more.

If you know where you are going to fish, it is easier to pick a rod specifically for your needs by using the regular guidelines. But if you are going to backpack through the Bob Marshal Wilderness and will be fishing unknown waters of varying size, it is best to get a basic rod and make do. When I'm heading for the backcountry, I usually take along extra lines in sizes heavier than my rod uses. Sometimes you'll find conditions requiring an extra-long cast or an extra-large fly. For the most part, it's okay to overload a glass rod occasionally, for angling emergencies.

On a bicycle trip from Missoula to Yellowstone Park a few years ago, I took a four-piece, 7-foot Leonard Duracane, an impregnated rod made for the company in England. It took a No. 4 line and was fine for the upper Big Hole and other smaller waters, but when we got to the Park, I was outclassed by the big rivers. I was also worried about the Leonard riding on the fragile luggage carrier. I had fantasies that it would fall off in front of a truck.

As a special present to myself last year, I had Russ Peak build what I consider the ultimate traveling rod. It is a four-piece, 8-foot glass one that takes a No. 6 line—my basic rod for freshwater use. But, aside from the fantastic workmanship and love Peak lavishes on his glass, this rod is special: at my request, he duplicated the action of my bamboo Para 15—my regular rod. Though an admitted luxury, this was a fine idea; for me, the Paul Young semi-parabolic has the best action I've yet encountered, and to have the same general feel in glass gives me the option of leaving the Young home on some trips. I had a metal-and-leather case made for my Peak rod that covers the original aluminum case and hooks onto my North Face Pack. It is a powerful rod, capable of long casts with a weight-forward line, and yet can delicately handle a double-tapered, too. It is so nice that at times I use it for regular fishing—especially in the spring or on rainy days when I get nervous about bamboo. But $150 is a lot of money for a pack rod, and most sensible people wouldn't spend it that way. I travel a lot on trains and busses and take the Peak whether I'm going to New York in December or Livingston in August. With reinforced glass ferrules ringed with metal, it is trustworthy and doesn't compromise quality.

For regular backpacking, I don't use the metal-and-leather case because it weighs too much. I recommend that you replace yours with a plastic case that can be found commercially or made from plastic tubing available at agricultural implement stores. Such a case offers adequate protection and saves nearly a pound, which you appreciate after 20 miles.

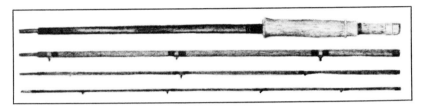

Russ Peak pack rod made for Harmon Henkin,
four-piece, 8-foot glass, No. 6 line

If you're planning a very long trip, say Europe or South America, with your possessions on your back, there is one trick you might consider. Some of the custom builders like Peak, Powell or Winston might make you a back-up blank. If you are fishing 2,000 miles from civilization (i.e., from a rodmaker) and your sole rod gives up the ghost, you're up the creek without a paddle, so to speak. But if you've had your favorite builder put up a four-piece blank that fits nicely in the rear of your pack, another section (or whole rod) can be easily finished on the spot. It isn't difficult to improvise a handle if you carry a few small tools along and have the fittings from your broken rod to work with. This semiduplicate can be a time and money saver, without representing a great expense. The blank should be as close as can be to your main pack rod's action, made from the same mandrel if possible, so that the pieces are interchangeable.

As another aside, when I'm heading for remote geographic areas I always take a few dozen interesting patterns such as Sculpins and outrageous nymphs. They make nice presents when

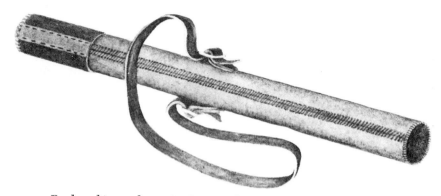

Backpacking rod case for Russ Peak pack rod made for Harmon Henkin

trying to make friends in new places. Fishermen around the world like these trinkets, no matter if they fish with No. 20's and you're giving them a 4/0 tarpon fly. It's the thought that counts.

CADDIS A LA WRIGHT RODS

When Wright's *Fishing the Dry Fly as a Living Insect* came out a few years back, it was hailed as an important book. As such things go, it was probably the most important and best-written fly-fishing book for a couple of decades. Certainly it was about time someone recognized the real significance of the caddis and grappled with the long-surviving dogma, established by Frederick Halford in the nineteenth century, of the upstream, dead-drift cast.

Along with the significance of the caddis fly, Leonard Wright had some opinions on tackle. He really sounded the bugle for the first major assault on the doctrine of shortness that had been sweeping the country since the early 1960's. He carried his argument to the point of favoring the use of those long willowy rods that were the accepted length in the early part of the century. His reasons for not liking short sticks were simple. With them, you can't control as much line, or your fly, and you can't keep enough line off the water. Undeniably true, but I still haven't seen many people swap their ultralights for weepy Leonards and Thomases over 9 feet that take No. 4 and No. 5 lines. His logic did impress enough anglers to start a minor and short-lived boom on these rods in stores with used tackle.

For certain kinds of fishing, these rods are very fine—and not only for giving a Wright caddis that "sudden inch." If you can get into their gentle rhythms, they are fun for fishing two or three wet flies, as anglers did in the nineteenth century. However, despite Wright's penchant for them, you shouldn't expect miracles. They aren't for what I call hypermodern anglers, with our exact-replication nymphs, minnows and large dries. You won't find the control required for long or quick casts.

They also seem to me to be top-heavy and woody for anglers with our current sensibilities. Dick Eggert has a venerable 10-foot Leonard that he sometimes uses in this way, but even he tires of it after a while. There are plenty of current rods that will do the caddis job satisfactorily, including some glass ones. The main properties required are a length of at least 8½ feet and a line no weightier than No. 5. You minimize drag this way while maximizing control. Twitch fishing isn't all that difficult once you get into it. Remember that the lighter the line, the better you'll do.

TAKE IT AND LAKE IT

The only thing to really emphasize in still-water trout rods, called "reservoir rods" by our English cousins, is that extra length is often a bonus. In this fishing, you will either cast for cruising fish you can see or be tossing into the great beyond. Unless the wind requires a heavier one, you can get away with very light lines, depending on fly size. Bulky sinking lines seem to have a knack of hopelessly wrapping around various underwater objects. A long rod will enable you to keep more line off the water, which is handy while playing fish as well as in working the fly.

Lake fishing is pretty slow, since your fly is left to float or you endure a long wait while it sinks, except when there is a hatch and the activity is on the surface. Since there is so much standing and holding time in lake fishing, rod weight can be a factor for an all-day affair. You will want to consider this in your choice.

In lakes where monsters are sometimes intercepted, big flies are the rule. In others I've fished, the trout were partial to No. 16's and smaller. Other than this, general rules of rod selection hold.

One more thing about lakes—beware of trolling, even in a canoe. It's something you should never do with a fine rod unless you are rich and foolhardy.

At the beginning of the 1974 season Wynn Rainbolt and I tried Seeley Lake for rainbows, having heard mysterious rumors of large fish in this medium-sized lake along the Swan Range. Wynn had moved to Montana recently from New England and was an expert canoeist. We cast big streamers and nymphs for hours along the windy shoreline of the lake from a canoe, without a strike. Then we had the bright idea of trolling, with a sinking line and a marabou muddler. As we drifted rapidly along, a mighty fish swatted my fly, doubling the rod over, as they say in the outdoor mags. I missed the fish and immediately hooked and lost another one. I landed the third one, a brutish bull trout (the local name for Dolly Varden) over 7 pounds, after a major-length battle. I lost one again and then grabbed onto a monster. We fought desperately for a little while, but the brute cracked my Orvis below the ferrule, alas.

It was the second 9-foot, 6-ounce Shooting Star I have broken in my life. Undoubtedly a record for breaking Shooting Stars! Wynn hadn't had a strike on his floating line, but he didn't have a broken rod either. When big fish hit a fast-moving streamer, they hit it hard. The rod can't give as it does when you are stationary, so it suffers incredible pressure. It doesn't take any delicacy to drag a fly while drifting in a raft or canoe, so don't risk a good rod without a reason.

GARBAGE

I'll come right out and admit it. Always in the deep recesses of my vest or kit bag there is one solitary hook—naked to the world. No feathers, no furs and not even a smidgin of polypropylene. It's a bait hook, plain and simple. I haven't used it for years, but you never know.

Now this will offend some refined sensibilities, but there are lots of things a fly outfit will do well besides casting a fly. Ask any old-timer who fished before the invasion of the spinning rod. Our gentle fly rods work well with various baits, small spinners and even tiny plugs. The stores used to be full of such goodies.

This is a hard thing to do to a beloved rod, but for those who feel motivated . . . well, that's up to you. My old Maryland fishing buddy, Peter Streett, had a giant battery of wooden rods which he believed were created, basically, to roll cast nightcrawlers. It was truly an awesome sight to watch as with a quick downward jerk the 9-foot rod would form a big hoop in the A-level line, rolling the lowly worm 60 feet.

If you sometimes fall from grace in this manner, you should do it with a stoutish rod—glass if possible. Those little fly-rod plugs and spinners can be harsh on your light tackle. If you have the tendency, don't feel bad about dragging a worm through a holeful of finny creatures. Some of the new-wave nymphs, which are being advertised everywhere these days, are as heavily weighted as any of the old-time spinners and plugs. They can be very hazardous to your health when false casting, however, since they always seem attracted to your head. Either roll cast them or let them slowly out downstream.

I once asked the publisher of a would-be "fancy" fly-fishing magazine if I could do a short piece on "alternate uses of the fly rod." From the look he gave me I might just as well have asked if I could be a centerfold in the mag, stark naked, holding a Leonard Fairy reel between my teeth.

Good luck and don't tell anyone that I mentioned it!

14

Reels

One of the greater myths of fly-fishing is that the reel is merely a place to store line. After I'd accepted this notion for years, one day the bubble burst. I had just met a charming artist-writer named Russ Chatham who had migrated to the Livingston area of Montana after breaking the world striped-bass-on-a-fly record with a 36-pound beast from San Francisco Bay.

We were sitting in his yard, swapping introductory fish tales, and I showed him the battery of fancy rods that I was lugging around. He seemed politely impressed but questioned me carefully on my reels. Reels! What the hell. How could they compare to my beloved rods? I had two Hardy Lightweights and a Scientific Angler System 8. Wasn't that good enough to store line?

I brushed past his questions to ask him about his rods. I figured that, as an old-line West Coaster, he would have at least a couple of bamboo rods, perhaps a Winston and a Powell and probably a Russ Peak custom glass. He didn't have any of that stuff. He was basically a steelhead, salmon and striper fisherman. For his Montana trouting he used a home-built, 7½-foot bamboo rod. For the big-league fishing, especially steelhead, he used funny 9-foot glass rods that took lines ranging from No. 8 to No. 10, depending on his mood and water conditions. He put these rods together from the least expensive Fenwick blanks ($2 each at the time), sleazy reel seats and coarsely wrapped or even taped guides. This guy was definitely not a rod purist when fishing seriously.

He picked up one of my rods, a large Paul Young, and gently cast out the entire WF No. 9. He had never used a parabolic or semiparabolic before, but instantly mastered it. I realized this was a no-joke angler, serious about the sport, so I questioned him about reels. What is their rightful place in the universe of tackle? I asked. Ah, now, there was a subject that brought a gleam to Russ's eyes. We went into his den and he started taking out reels and reels and reels and talking about them.

His favorites were the Hardy Perfects, sturdily built English reels made from roughly the 1890's to the early 60's and reissued tentatively in 1975. They have supersmooth-turning ball bearings but I had considered them too heavy. They have a side plate, a wonderful feature on any reel, that can be palmed to slow down a running fish. Then he produced a Vom Hofe, the legendary early American reel, which in the bigger sizes was his favorite salmon and saltwater choice. He had narrow-spooled Pfluegers that featured, because of their narrow design, a very quick retrieve; some Scientific Anglers, made by Hardy Brothers as a compromise between the Lightweight series and the old Perfects, not constructed as well as the Perfect but better than the Lightweight; a couple of St. Georges, with agate guides and a huge capacity for their size; a wondrous Bogdan, handmade in Nashua, New Hampshire, for a lot of money, but with a drag that operated with the slightest twist of a lever. There were others as well.

I began to take reels more seriously at that moment. They were no longer adjuncts to my rods, but became equal in importance, if not actually superior. Once I became vulnerable on the subject, Russ quickly pointed out the flaws in my previous notions. My beloved Hardy Lightweights were okay for light trouting, but couldn't cut it for big stuff. They were too fragile, something I had noticed but overlooked the few times in the past that I had dropped one on a streamside rock. The Lightweights also have no dragging system, aside from the puny screw on the side that merely adjusts the tension on the line. Now, I partially agree with some of the forthcoming objections to these comments about Lightweights and similar reels. It is rare for an angler to need a functioning break. On the other hand, when you really need a drag, there is nothing, but nothing, that will take its place. And the larger the fish you are after the more important the quality of the reel becomes, and things like a drag are critical. Trout fishermen usually take the luxury of picking their reels because of aesthetics and other considerations, such as the sound of the click.

There are two general ways to look at fishing, though we

usually blend them. It can be seen as a series of events given their deepest meaning through the exceptional happening—taking a big fish. Most trophy fishermen view the sport in this way. The only thing that really counts is the monster. Everything else is preparatory and emotionally irrelevant. The other way to view fly-fishing is as a whole organic process, intimately connected within itself, wherein no single moment has a greater significance than the process of fishing as a whole.

What do those philosophical ramblings have to do with reels and drags? Simple. Though I am trying to avoid cluttering this book with Me and Joe fish stories, one or two might be illustrative.

One evening I was fishing a grand stretch of the upper Clark Fork River, near Missoula. This water, despite the ravages of the Anaconda Company's copper smelter, the Highway Department and some minor sewage dumping, is a great place to while away the hours in search of brown trout. It was late summer, and small brown caddis were hatching plentifully. Even the biggest fish were interested in surface feeding. I had been fishing this water almost every night during August and doing very well—well enough to have cavalierly thrown back a 4-pounder. (These details are always important in Me and Joe stories, aren't they?)

This particular evening I made a long cast to the other bank, 60 feet away. A monster trout, as the outdoor writers say, et my fly. The berserk brown made a long run, going way into my backing, headed downstream. As it semipaused in mid-river for a few moments, I managed to retrieve about half the line. When it got bored with the waiting game, it ran again, taking all my line and backing with it. I felt and heard that heartrending snap, and it was free.

I've taken a 6-pound brown from the Big Hole and have also felt good-sized rainbows and whatevers on my rod. But this was a granddaddy and must have gone 10 pounds—no kidding. (One great advantage of Me and Joe fish stories is that the reader has to take the writer's word.) When I collapsed on the bank, pipe chattering in my teeth, I pondered man's fate and reel design and construction. I had been using my 8-foot Paul Young Para 15, a sturdy stick, and my favorite trout reel, a medium-sized Walker. The Walker is a lovely New York–made reel, finely constructed, nice-sounding and classically designed, all of which appeals to me very much. Right now it sells for $100 new, and mine had always served me well. But for this fish it was the wrong piece of machinery. Without a drag and with nothing to grab at except its big

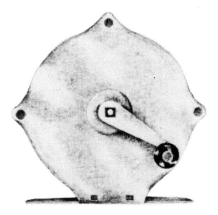

Dame Stoddard & Kendall brass trout reel, $1 in 1890

handle, when that bozo brown started its long march I couldn't
stop it without resorting to Izaak Walton's trick of throwing the rod
on the water and following it. As everyone who has had a similar
experience sadly knows, it is quite difficult—nay, impossible—to
clutch a handle whirling around at fantastic speed, even if you
are willing to sacrifice a few knuckles. (In 1975, after numerous
queries and complaints, Walker began adding a drag system to
some of their reels.)

At home I had a Fin-Nor No. 1, a scaled-down model of the
famous saltwater reel. It is practically indestructible, inside and
out. This number costs over $125 and is encased in an ultramodern
stainless-steel package. It is a very fine reel but heavy and so
modernistic that it will probably be given to astronauts when they
head for a planet with oceans. When I travel to unknown destina-
tions, I take this reel and an extra spool, since it can take at least
as much as I can. It is equipped with a drag that can be tight-
ened down easily, like a star drag, by turning a large knob to as
much resistance as you would need to stop a charging water
buffalo. It also has ball bearings, like the Hardy Perfect, to ensure
a smooth operation. If I had had the Fin-Nor that day, I could
have turned the drag to a point slightly short of snapping the 4X
tippet and made that fish work for every inch. I might even have
tired it enough to land it. But I don't like to use the Fin-Nor on a
regular basis. It is too heavy for its No. 6 capacity and looks peculiar as hell on a bamboo rod.

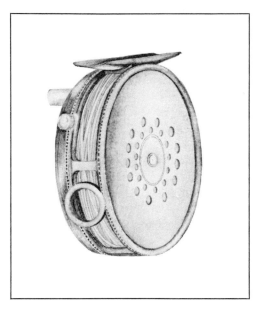

Early Hardy Perfect reel, circa 1920

I also have a Hardy Perfect, which could have been palmed to give me a better chance against the fish, and an old Cortland reel, made in England, that has a 2:1 retrieve ratio. With that, I could have picked up the line rapidly when the fish paused in its flight, considerably increasing my chance for success.

Nevertheless, even though I lost the biggest brown that will probably ever appear in my lifetime, I fish hundreds of hours each season and still prefer the Walker for most of them. If 10-pound browns were the rule rather than the dismal exception, I would use a more substantial reel. They aren't and I don't.

This is really a way of equivocating on the reel issue. I know many fine anglers who use nothing but Medalists, and most photos of such superstars as Ernie Schwiebert feature Hardy Light-weights, usually in the mid-capacity Princess model. There are some anglers who don't care what they have on the end of their rod. Joe Brooks seemed to prefer the old Johnson Magnetics, perhaps the smoothest-operating reels ever made. Some Japanese imitations of Hardys, marketed by Heddon and some others, are plenty good enough and very cheap.

There are a lot of reasons, however, why you should beware of those delectable-looking ultralight reels that are so delicately put together—no matter how fine they feel and how expensive they are. In the hands of someone who is reasonably careful with equipment and fishes where falls are unusual, they can last longer than the angler, but it takes just one mistake to put them out of business, for a while at least. My Orvis CFO, a fine new lightweight that's been coming out since the early 1970's, was an early victim of an untoward rock, which necessitated a return to the factory. Of course, there is a big difference between someone fishing relatively protected waters and myself, doing a ludicrous imitation of a mountain goat on the Big Hole Canyon rocks.

Reels are the least changed item of tackle. Charles Orvis put out the first perforated spool reel—perforated to lighten it and facilitate drying of silk lines—back in the 1870's. If you browse through turn-of-the-century or older catalogs you'll find Orvis frame reels, Leonard raised-frame models and Hardy Brothers Proto Perfects. If you are antique-minded, here is the one area where you can really indulge yourself. It isn't much fun to spend a streamside day lugging around a 10-foot Leonard or Hardy rod, with its willowy action, but a small old Leonard or Hardy reel works just as well as anything fresh off the shelf. There were also scores of lesser-known but fine machined reels, like Wilsons, Scribeners and Vom Hofes, made for other outfits, that can sometimes be picked up cheaply. You can occasionally find such reels for small change in antique or secondhand shops. They are sold for minifortunes by used tackle dealers, who are profitably raising old-brand-name consciousness among the masses. But the two Leonards, the Vom Hofe and the old Hardy cost me just a few bucks apiece. Patience, in lieu of wealth, is a virtue.

Just a word about automatic reels—you've undoubtedly heard this before—don't get one unless you really want it. On the other hand, there was the time I gave a snooty lecture in Missoula on choosing the proper tackle. I issued the obligatory warnings about automatic reels—how they have no room for backing, jam at inopportune times and are vastly overweight—and the audience of beginners took in my sage words; but in the back of the room

131

was an older fellow, decidedly unimpressed by my modernity. He ventured that in some fifty years of fishing western Montana, he had owned only four reels, all automatics. His Martins and Perrines had never hung up, had carried plenty of line for him and were not, he said, too heavy. I respectfully backed off.

I will readily admit their advantage in certain limited circumstances, like fishing from a boat for sunfish and small bass. When automatics were first introduced by the Martin Company, in the late nineteenth century, fly lines were generally level and silk, their diameter very thin. You could fit a hundred feet easily onto an auto. In those days fly-fishing was mostly done close in, with wet flies tossed out a short distance from the angler. Now we whippersnappers effortlessly cast 60 to 70 feet with bulky, synthetic lines that clog automatics. Manufacturers are trying to keep the basic convenient features of automatics, like being able to bring in 25 feet of line with a touch of the finger, but to adapt them to modern bulky fly lines. Evidently it hasn't been easy. However, you should always get a free stripping automatic, since they will continue to allow a fish to run even after the spring is fully wound—otherwise, *boing!*

This brings us to another aspect of the reel question—weight. I was nurtured in the school that believed in a reel balancing a rod. Now I'm not sure what that meant, aside from some metaphysical nonsense, like there being harmony in an angler watching a 6-pound fish snap off a 6X tippet. The old formula was that a reel should be 1½ times the weight of a rod for balance. A 4-ounce rod took a 6-ounce reel. But practically, one should operate within the bounds of common sense rather than by formulas. It must be admitted that a 10-ounce Hardy Perfect feels weird on a 2-ounce Thomas 6-footer. On such a rod, a Hardy Lightweight or Tiny Walker might feel and look better, but aside from these far-fetched examples, weight and balance are a moot point in choosing a reel. Scientific Anglers' idea of balanced rods and reels is sensible, but an extra ounce more or less wouldn't change the appropriateness much, especially if it means a better-built reel. The balance problem is that both thin and chubby hands go between the working part of the rod and reel. We used to try to balance the rod and reel at the top of the handle, like the scales of justice. If the two parts were roughly equal in weight, then we were using a just combination, but the weight of your hand, like the weight of the law and the court, intervenes and it becomes a silly equation.

It was my interest in the relatively heavy Hardy Perfects that made me rethink the balance issue. Those delights are usually a good 2 ounces heavier than the equal-capacity lightweights that I had been using, but are much better built. Instead of a 4-ounce Princess reel I began using a 6- or 7-ounce Perfect on my Para 15 4-ounce rod—big deal. I have really never felt the difference. If you are going to make a fetish of lightness, then go ahead with the CFO's, Lightweights and the like, but don't feel sacrilegious if the weightier models seem better to you. Take whatever seems right. There are no meaningful objective formulas.

This is especially true with the big reels for ocean flats, steelhead and salmon rivers and bass lakes. Specialized reels for this kind of work are expensive, but often outstanding examples of workmanship. Many get by with old standards like the Medalist for the light end of this fishing, but if you're after tarpon or other monsters, you should have more reel. This is where the Seamasters, Fin-Nors, big Walkers, Bogdans and their kin pay off. A fish that is going to run off a hundred yards of backing is the fish that will burn a friction drag apart and cause the reel to jam at a critical moment during the fight. Most flycasters don't need to be overly concerned with them.

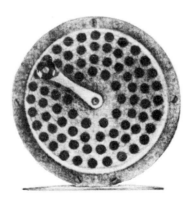

Historic Orvis trout reel: first perforated model

Tom McGuane and Guy Valdene do a lot of fishing in the Florida Keys. They are very partial to the Seamasters, but also use Bogdans and Scientific Angler System 12's. That kind of equipment, used under extreme pressures, becomes very personal—a subject of heated discussion between various partisans. If you're at this arcane end of saltwater fishing, your own opinions are undoubtedly firmly formed, and if you're just getting there, you will be subjected to fierce opinions anyway. But there is a pragmatism about this subject of big reels with gigantic capacities. If one ever screws you up, you'll never trust it again, no matter what the price and guarantee. In a situation where you may cast only a few times a day to behemoths you have spent baking hours in the sun stalking, you can't afford to worry about quality. It is too expensive a sport to worry about $50, more or less, for a reel. That amount won't hire a good guide in the Keys for half a day.

For a lot of the intermediate fishing, such as long casting on big rivers, bass bugging and going after medium-sized steelies, I like multiplying reels (those with winding ratio higher than 1:1) like the Bogdan 1/0 or the English reels marketed by Cortland and Gladding. Hardy also makes a fine line of multipliers in the Lightweight series that add surprisingly small amounts of weight to the standard model. Remember, though, if you hope to break a world record, that multipliers are not allowed.

Many of the adept consider multipliers an unnecessary luxury. But when tangles of line seem to grow out of your every cast, they can be awfully handy. They are also beneficial when playing a decent fish, though I don't like reels that have more than 2:1 retrieve ratios, as they seem to give me less control. A slight turn of the handle with a 3:1 or 4:1 reel puts too much pressure on the fish—pressure that should be on the long fly rod.

If you are using a reel with a friction drag, check it out carefully. When they go bad they tighten up as line is taken out. Grab the end and run a hundred yards quickly. You can undoubtedly use the exercise, and it is a good way to see how the braking system is working. The same sort of test can be done with light trout or panfish reels. Strip out some line and see how it sounds and feels. It should be smooth. Most of the silent drag reels, some made by Hardy and others by Pezon & Michel, aren't really too much. To me, the noise is an important part of the sense of fighting a big fish. Silence dulls things, whereas a whirring reel adds to my excitement.

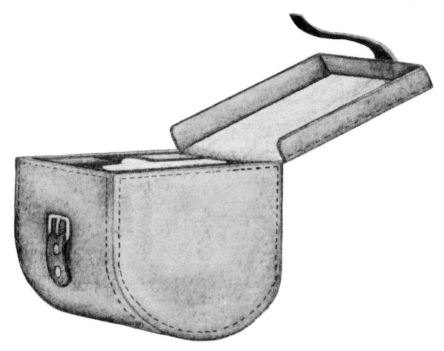

Hardy Perfect reel case

There is much less danger in buying a secondhand reel than a secondhand rod, even for the untutored. Bamboo rods are subject to a sea of trouble, as Hamlet said about life, and the intricacies of cane construction can hide a multitude of sins from the amateur. With reels, however, basically they work or they don't. Though collectors may get all warm and sticky over a virgin Perfect or Bogdan, for the practical angler a little wear isn't anything to be concerned about. There aren't too many possible mechanical defects. If the frame is bent you will notice it, and if the drag seems to work okay, it probably is.

The following list is basically my observations on the current reel market and is not definitive. It will provide a place to start bargaining, and bargaining is what secondhand buying should be about. The list is for reels in fine to excellent shape, meaning that the reel hasn't been obviously abused, everything works and it looks nice. A little of the finish being worn off is acceptable, but if any irregularities beyond that exist, you should start driving the price down. Some of the current reel fetishism has bloated prices out of line for some models like the Perfects, but if you want one, that won't stop you.

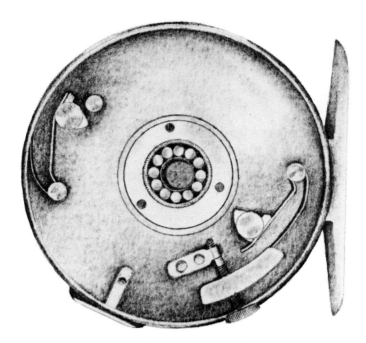

Inside of early Hardy Perfect reel, circa 1920

Sometimes it is difficult to tell the nineteenth-century and early-twentieth-century bait-casting reels from fly reels. Distinctions as they are known today did not always exist. Check out the line capacity carefully. If you can't tell which kind of reel it is but it will do your job, it really doesn't matter. If you do find that it is an early bait reel, you should pay a little less, but buy it and use it anyway.

The following makes of reels are listed in ascending order of value, except for the Hardys leading off because of their very wide range of models.

HARDYS

Lightweights—$25–$40. The standard high-quality reels of the past couple of decades. They have replaced the Perfect, St. George and the like for most anglers. Made from very lightweight alloy, they range in capacity from the minuscule Flyweight to the huge Husky, suitable for heavy steelheading and salmon. Favored by many anglers who could afford anything, they are truly excellent reels.

St. Georges and St. Johns—$40–$60. Fine quality, perforated spool, traditional reels which probably were the forerunners of the current Lightweights, but better made. They have big capacities and are favored for salmon and steelhead by some. The agate guide can crack, so look at it carefully. The St. John is being made again, but it's not quite as nice.

Perfects—$50–$100. Top-quality side plate reels, made for fifty years until about 1965. They are really smooth, utilizing ball bearings, and were made in sizes from small trout to giant salmon in all diameters. Their only drawback is weight (a little heavy), which isn't much of a factor. They are very sturdy and prized by collectors and hoarders.

Hardy also made many other models, ranging from the nice little Uniqua, a relatively inexpensive but fine reel, to the so-called Tobique River, a big salmon copy of the Vom Hofe. Just about anything marked by Hardy will be fine to very fine and usually expensive.

Fin-Nor No. 1 reel, for trout

PFLEUGER MEDALIST

$5–$10. As American as a Chevrolet, but better made, Medalists have been *the* reel for just regular folks for years. The best of the bunch are the older narrow-spool models.

STREAMCRAFT

$15. Fine New Zealand imitation of the Hardy Perfect, complete down to the bearings. A nice trinket if you find anyone heading down under.

PEZON & MICHEL

$20. Perhaps you should pass up this French-made reel. This was one of Charlie Ritz's brainstorms. It turned out to be a drizzle.

PFLEUGER GREAT WEST

$25. Made in the 20's and 30's, with German silver and hard rubber. They are top-quality trouting reels.

FARLOW

$25. Fine English-made reel with adjustable drag. The Sapphires were imitations of the Hardy Lightweights and close in quality.

Heddon-imported Japanese imitation of
Hardy reel mounted on custom-made reel seat

YOUNG

$25. English-built and imported by Garcia, among others, in the past. Their Pridex and Beaudex were at least as well made as the Hardy Lightweights, for less money. The dual-handled Beaudex is a good reel in the medium sizes. They also made a good side plate reel, but it isn't around much anymore.

WILSON

$25. Good quality, like the Pfleuger Great West.

BOUGLE

$25 up. Made in Alnwich, England, as Hardys are. More obscure, but a good-quality piece of equipment.

TALBOT

$25 up. Ben Hur is a small, very pretty German silver reel from around the 1920's, of Vom Hofe quality. They are difficult to obtain, and it's unlikely you'd find one.

SCRIBENER

$25. Another obscure but good-quality, hard-rubber-sided reel, that is sometimes available secondhand at bargain rates.

ORVIS

$40. The skeletal CFO's sound and look good, but are at least a tad on the fragile side. Among the lower-priced works, the Orvis Battenkill multipliers built by Young of England and the Madison reels are better buys if they can be found secondhand.

MEEK

$50. The early ones that were made by this company were superb and primarily known for baitcasting. The later ones are very fine, but not quite as appealing as the older ones.

139

Pfleuger Medalist reel, for small trout

FIN-NOR

$75 up. Space-age technology and my robot's favorite reels. They are golden-colored, alas, but undeniably sturdily built, with a top-quality drag. The little trout No. 1 is heavy for most use and has a sorry capacity. For salt water, the Big Bears are great.

VOM HOFE

$75 up for authenticated ones. The Payne of the reel world, made in every size from tiny to huge ocean models. Just about the ultimate quality available, they are drooled after by collectors. Vom Hofe made bunches of reels under all sorts of other brand names in the same way as Heddon did with rods. Sometimes bargains can be found, but you have to look for the Vom Hofe quality.

Trout-sized Walker reel, 1972

WALKER

$60 for trout, $90 for salmon. They are fine reels, supposedly in the tradition of the Zwargs and the Vom Hofes, but the new ones for $100 aren't as fine as older top-quality reels. It would also be better if they had some sort of drag, a feature available for a bit more money. They are about the best trout reels being sold today, but they have lots of competition in the salmon area.

LEONARD

$100. They made a whole line of reels from the delicate Fairy reels (for their Baby Catskill rod, which weighs an ounce) to bigger models for whatever you care to hook. They are among the best reels ever made, and prized possessions.

BOGDAN

$100 up. Ultrafine, handcrafted, big multiplying reels for salmon, steelhead and saltwater use. They have the nicest drag I've ever seen, which works with the slightest pressure on the lever. Big, no doubt, but as nice a reel as they make these days.

HEWITT

$???. Primo-quality ecstasy put out in rare, rare quantities by Edward Ringwood Hewitt, the dean of much twentieth-century American fly-fishing. This umptimillionaire could make the best and did. If you ever find one for sale, call me collect anytime.

Of course, this list barely scratches the surface of the used reel market for both current items and old-timers. There are scads of reels available today as in the past. Just look at some good ones to get a feel for the standards of quality involved before leaping in with dollars.

15

Lines

For some things, new is definitely better, and fly lines are one of those things. I am a bit suspicious of those who continue to eulogize and prefer silk lines, even for small dries. It's the same suspicion that flows automatically when someone says that they long for the "good old days" when ignorance, disease and superstition were even more common than they are now. There were some nice things that happened a hundred years ago, sure, especially looking at it from our present environmental morass. And there are some nice things to say about silk—but you can't take it too far.

As I have said before, lines are more crucial to modern fly-fishing than rods, reels and whatevers. They are the central ingredient in the evolution of tackle. You can cast 80 feet or so with a broom handle, but try to cast 50 feet with your new Berkeley and a horsehair line or even a wispy I-level silk line from the old days. Difficult at best, probably impossible.

Tapered lines seem to have first come to public notice somewhere in the 1870's, but they were probably around before then. Frederick Halford, the first dry-fly systematizer, discusses their importance in his 1889 book, *Dry Fly Fishing*. He stresses the use of pure silk, boiled in oil and tapered very carefully. In his aristocratic way, he reproached most manufacturers for turning out an inferior product and told his fellow gentlemen how to get the real thing. It's just as well that he doesn't have to put up with some of the modern tackle manufacturers' products!

Halford was in favor of a heavy line to buck the English breezes. He also insisted that split-cane rods were superior to wooden ones because they could handle heavier lines and were therefore easier to cast. Of course the greatly increased power-to-weight ratio of our current rods had not been reached. In a way the plaited silk lines lauded by Halford were more revolutionary than the change from natural to synthetic lines in the 1950's. It was the silk tapered line that allowed fly-fishing, in all its facets, to become what it is today. This was a change in kind, not just in quality.

These first silk lines were very similar to the ones still being made. The process of refinement came along very subtly—despite the manufacturers' claims of "new, improved" lines every year. Actually it has only been very recently, with silicone treatments during manufacture, that the silk line has become easier to use. No matter what claims writers make for silk lines, they are still a lot of bother—and are terrifically expensive. In 1975, King Eider silks list for about $35, and the few others still being made retail in the same category. In addition to this expense, they must be treated and dried after each use and have a tendency to gunk up without meticulous care. A silk caster also has to treat his line a few times during a day's fishing to keep it floating.

I know that some specialists, like Leonard Wright, love these traditional lines, and it's true that silk lines, in the lighter sizes, are incredibly smooth and seem to fit well with the mood of a lovely old bamboo rod. But unless you have special reason, they are definitely not worth the bother. If you are going to give it a whirl, use the very best like an Eider or a Transpar, the brand the Leonard featured. They are fine lines and will keep your worries to a minimum. You can graciously retire your silk after a few episodes and feel a bit traditional for the experience. The cheaper silks have a tendency to become like noodles, then weaken and rot. You can often pick up these high-grade silks cheap, or even free, from older anglers who went through their silk phase and now know better.

I'm going to back up a little and admit there are a few uses for old silk lines. One of them is as a sinking line, undressed or naked, as it were. They flow slowly downward at a pace that is often perfect for pond and shallow lake fishing with a nymph or wet fly. They can also be very handy in situations like some spring-creek fishing where drag is of importance. With a diameter that is far smaller than modern synthetics of comparable weight, they don't displace as much water. This feature can also be handy for bucking a wind, because they offer less resistance. All in all, though, you will pay an enormous price for these slight advantages.

Line greaser for silk lines

Once they gunk up, they are a problem, and many of the silk lines that have been offered to me are in this shape. Eggert has a whole box of silk lines received as gifts and in minor trades, covered with eons of dressing that has accumulated like mud on a slow wheel. Year after year he makes vague promises to clean them up during the off season, but I always notice a Cortland 444 on his reel when he gets down to serious fishing.

Edward Ringwood Hewitt, from the Standard Oil and U.S. Steel families, was the dominant figure in American angling, at least on the East Coast, after the passing of George LaBranche and Theodore Gordon. He devised a method of cleansing silk lines. The above background is thrown in because you should appreciate the irony of one of the wealthiest people in the nation stooping to hustling gunked-up fly lines from friends in order to clean them. When fellow club members threw away their plaited silk lines as unusable, he would grab them, clean them thoroughly and sell them back. Very enterprising.

He stretched the lines and rubbed them down with a mixture of pumice and linseed oil until they were as smooth as possible. Then he placed the clean line in linseed oil that had been boiled and purified for a couple of hours and slightly cooled. Next the line was stretched again and rubbed down once more with pumice and oil. After it dried, he stored it in scads of talcum powder to keep it in good shape. The method seems to work even without his drastic alternative, carbon tetrachloride application after the first pumicing if the first method failed. Carbon tet is a very dangerous poison, and its fumes can be lethal, so I would not recommend using it.

Anyway, if that fashionable millionaire Hewitt went to such extremes to clean his silk lines, we certainly should not expect less trouble.

It is very difficult to figure out the size of a silk line if there is no record of it. Despite a sizing system built around diameter, there was often a large disparity between the various brands. The best thing to do if you have a no-name silk line is to weigh it. In an ultimate sense, the diameter of a silk line isn't as important as its weight anyway. Just put the first 30 feet of the line on an accurate scale of the sort used for reloading ammunition or weighing out illegal substances. Using the chart, you can quickly tell what it will fit, but you'll often find that it is a No. 4½ or a No. 6¼, and then the problem is your own.

The weighing system of gauging lines took over from the diameter system during the early 1960's, when the American Fishing Tackle Manufacturer's Association looked the field over and decided it was a mess. The broad introduction of synthetic lines, ranging from finely made ones to rejected clotheslines, made the diameter system hopelessly obsolete. The diameters of synthetics ranged wildly, and a procedure based on weight was substituted. Despite the reactions of some of the faithful, who figure that if it's a change it must be bad, the new number system slowly took over. Today many anglers could not tell you what HEH or HDH means.

The 1950's and early 60's were an amazing time for synthetic lines. Most of them were so abysmal, like their ill-conceived glass-rod counterparts, it is no wonder that a few anglers continue to turn their noses up at everything but silk. I've seen some from this transitional phase and am very glad I never had to use one. From the end of the war until Scientific Anglers put out the first quality synthetics in the late 50's, companies deluged the market each year with their "Wondrous, superfloating, new synthetic, silklike, needs no dressing, ultimate fly lines," and they were all duds. But Scientific Anglers, starting out as a small company in Midland, Michigan, finally produced a good hollow-core line that did in fact float high and long, though admittedly the tip almost always sinks. At first these lines were a rich mahogany color and seemed to last almost forever. Dick Eggert still has a Scientific Angler Supreme from 1964 that is in good shape.

One of the next developments was the introduction of the white or light-colored line that was supposedly less visible than the dark colors. It makes sense. The fish is usually looking up at the fly and line with the light sky as a background. Dark stands out against light, eh? But many anglers went through the roof at these white and peach-colored lines. Maybe it offended their angling masculinity! The battle line was severely drawn for a few years over this issue. It was horrible enough to them when these plastic-covered things replaced silk but, as if that wasn't bad enough, they resembled spaghetti noodles—*hrumphh!* Incidentally, the idea for these lines supposedly came from some crackerjack British undersea commander during World War II. He mentioned to an angler over a hot toddy or something that white hulls were the hardest to spot from undersea. The angler got to thinking about this and light lines emerged.

For underwater use I still prefer dark-colored lines, since the fish see them against a darkened background, and almost all manufacturers indulge this somber taste among anglers. But, to be really brutal, I don't think the color business makes a helluva lot of difference. It seems to be one of those idiosyncratic things that keep arguments flaming so that fishermen have to worry less about getting skunked, whatever color line they use. The dark lines appeal more to some people's aesthetic sense. Others like white and for some the peach is best. Dale Pritchard, a long time western Montana angler and fly-tying instructor, ran some tests on the Bitterroot River and concluded that from dawn to dark the peach color is most visible to the angler. You can do with that what you will. It isn't worth climbing the barricades about.

Something that is important to a versatile angler is to take advantage of the great variety of line types available. When I got heavily into fly-fishing in the early 1960's, there were floating lines and sinking lines, and that was it. The full-length sinkers were a major bother for me to use, especially with good equipment. You could just feel a rod groaning over the burden of lifting 50 feet of line from the bottom of a stream. Dick and I built fishing ethics around the avoidance of sinking lines, except for dire emergencies, and at one time we were pompous enough to declare that the use of them was closer to spinning than fly-fishing. But things changed, both our attitudes and the lines themselves. First came the lines that sank slowly, then intermediately, then quickly—and finally, the ones that sank like a rock.

This was a significant step, but they were still complete sinkers. Then the sink-tip lines came on the scene, then the sink heads and now the sink bellies. Will wonders never cease? For most of my use of nymphs and streamers, I prefer high-density 10-foot section sink-tip lines. Except for some placid ponds, the regular slower-sinking tips don't seem to work as well. It takes forever and a day to get them down where you want the fly. Even in the Madison and other big waters, the high-density sink tips work well. I have also become a minor devotee of the sink-head line for big lakes, late-season river fishing with monster flies and even for some steelheading. The ones put out by Cortland and Scientific do their job very well, and it is a real advantage for me to have only 30 feet sink and have floating line behind it to ease the retrieve. The intermediate 20-foot sinking-belly lines seem to have a promising future as well, but it would be a bit embarrassing to lug along a sink tip, a sink belly, a sink head and a full sinking line. For everything in Montana, a sink tip and sink head will suffice, and for most trouting in the East, a sink tip is all you need.

For some fishing, like big steelheading, some transplanted saltwater cohos in the Great Lakes and similar endeavors, these halfway submergibles won't do the job. You'll need a whole sinker or even a shooting head to get the job done right.

Head fishing is a thing unto itself. Though for most anglers, 30 feet of fly line and 300 feet of monofilament are scarcely the most graceful outfit, in the hands of longtime practitioners it can work very, very well. The first time I fished with California rod builder Russ Peak, he used an assortment of his small rods with very light shooting heads. He handled No. 4, No. 5 and No. 6 heads with flat Cobra Monofilament shooting line remarkably smoothly. He used a small deerhair dry fly that he had tied, and his casts landed on the water very gracefully. Peak uses heads to test his rods, feeling that this is the most accurate way to see how the rods handle the appropriate lines. Thirty feet of line is the standard measurement to balance line and rod, and Peak is exceedingly precise.

Some of the other shooters I know, notably Russ Chatham, can also handle that relatively light monofilament backing as if it were rope. But it is a time-consuming process to learn. If you think it can be picked up overnight, you'll experience some of the worst bird's nests imaginable. For some fishing, shooting heads are the simplest way to go. If you are going to be making long, rhythmic casts all day, it is much simpler to pick up 30 feet of line, false-cast it once, double-haul it and let it go. In the hands of an expert it has a pace of its own.

Until recently, heads were pretty much the province of West Coast steelheaders, who made their own by cutting down lines.

Recently Cortland and others have got into manufacturing them in various weights, both floating and sinking. It is usual to back them with regular round nylon about 20- to 30-pound test, but many people, like Peak, prefer the flat monofilament. It shoots better, is less apt to tangle and more easily untangles if your plans go awry.

There is one other way to go through the comedy of learning to use them—the use of the floating so-called running line. This thin No. 1 line is spliced onto the end of the shooting head. You let the heavy 30 feet through the guides and shoot away, the head pulling the running line. It doesn't work quite as well as the monofilament for distance, but it makes it a lot simpler to get into heads, being easier to handle and untangle. You can work your way up to nylon from these 100-foot spools of level fly line. I have also used No. 2 and No. 3 level lines for making improvised heads. I find that this chunkier line holds up the shooting head a little better, though the thinner the backing line the more distance you get.

I haven't used heads enough to become proficient in handling very thin nylon backing. I suspect there are more people like myself around than admit it. Those who are proficient with them invariably favor a hand retrieve with the line wrapped between the fingers. For the next cast, they put the backing between their lips and release it when they shoot. This works well for those who have mastered it, but those who wrap too tightly around their fingers or chomp down on it are in for trouble.

It is sometimes difficult to overcome the common habit of allowing fly line to accumulate around your feet when using normal short casts and full fly lines, but this will certainly result in all sorts of grade-B tragedies for the head user. Fifty feet of nylon around your feet is as bad as a salmon in a gill net. A shooting basket is a big help for me when using heads and wading deep. I just let the line fall into the basket and accumulate. It works all right, but not as well as a real mastery of the head techniques.

Shooting baskets of canvas are another bit of tackle getting very expensive, nearly $15. I don't suppose that's a surprise. They can be made in a pinch from a small cardboard box held around your waist with a belt or the like. A longer-lasting one can be made from one of those light plastic food containers that the stores are full of. I used one like that for a few seasons but became self-conscious about it. That green mottled plastic thing in front of me made me look like a traveling bait salesman or as if my casting was so bad I threw up a lot.

149

Shooting basket for long casts

The extreme of sinking lines and shooting heads are the lead cores, made from the metal-centered trolling line favored by lake trout anglers. You can cut off as much line as necessary to meet your weight requirements. They are level, but work well when the circumstances require it. I recently saw a fine English tackle-supply house offering lead cores for sale, so they can't be that crude. For many steelheading and ocean situations they will mean the difference between success and failure. But never use good rods with them, as they wear down tackle very quickly. If you are going to that length to catch fish, use a makeshift rod from a cheap blank. There is no false casting with lead cores anyway; you just pull back and let it go. A false cast is useless, and dangerous besides. I have seen nasty forehead cuts on anglers who had a momentary lapse of memory while using a lead-core line. Their weight drags them by you at head level on every false cast, and you have to build up your own simple pace of pickup to avoid the fear and trembling that often accompany their use.

A handy reserve line, if you can still find one, are those Scientific Angler variable-weight jobs—Vari-Lines—that have a different intermediate weight on either end. They had some that were light on one end and middleweight on the other. Another model was intermediate on one end and heavy on the other. In a pinch they can substitute for a broken line, something that has happened to me only once. I had been fishing the Bitterroot with a brand-new line that got caught between two jagged rocks and broke at the belly when I foolishly tugged it hard. It ruined a day's fishing, and since then I have one of those Vari-Lines tucked away in the back of my vest. Now, if I or any fishing chum needs a line in a pinch, it'll be there. It's hard to keep an exact selection of backup emergency lines with you if you aren't sure what line weight you'll be using on a given day. These lines were made for unskilled rookies, but work all right even for the refined.

Here I go into another touchy area—weight forward and double taper. I can't expect to win on this either way, but I will spell out my preferences. I use a double taper for Nos. 3, 4, 5 and usually 6, but use a weight forward from No. 7 upward. The difference in presentation is really not that significant for a good caster, even with light lines, but I won't claim to have all the answers. For many years, I even used a No. 4 weight forward, but over the past two seasons I have mellowed somewhat. Dick, who despises weight-forward lines, believes they are just another example of the modern sensibility and not worth discussing. I'm not so sure. Though I don't consider myself an example of finesse, there have only been a couple of times when fishing flies as small as a No. 20 with a weight-forward line that I wished for a double taper. Maybe the splash factor isn't as significant as the classicists claim.

It seems that single, short-tapered, weight-forward lines were primarily a salmon-fishing outgrowth of the double-tapered lines pioneered by Colonel Monel near the turn of the century. It was universally acknowledged in those days that weight-forward lines were much cruder, but they were handy for long casts in salmon fishing. Then bass buggers with their big cork flies picked them up and then saltwater fishing and so on. They moved to trout mainly through power fishing in the 60's. The basic difference between the two types of lines is the abruptness of the taper. The double starts slow, builds up to the belly of the line and then works its way symmetrically back at the end of the line. The weight forward's thin-end section is shorter and builds up quickly to a fat belly and then drops off abruptly to small again. It isn't reversible. The double taper can be used as two lines by switching ends, a money-saving thing.

Modern double-tapered lines are designed pretty much the way that they have always been. Weight forwards are now more subtle than they were originally, with longer lead-ins to the body, eliminating some of their old coarseness. You'll have to make the ultimate decision about how much coarseness they've managed to overcome. In my role as unofficial teacher, I've always recommended that people begin with a weight forward, as they are much easier to learn how to cast with. The relative gentleness of doubles is a taste that can be acquired as the beginner develops skill and technique. The claim made by some people that a double is better for all anglers isn't reasonable.

If you're making long casts consistently, then a weight forward is best. For dry flying or light nymphing with small flies and casts under 25 feet, by all means use a double taper. Give them both a try with as little preconception as possible. Here again you'll have to compromise between the ease of bucking winds and handling outsized flies with a weight forward and the delicacy of a double. Nothing is perfect, as they say, and that applies especially to fly tackle.

There are actually a lot of similar types of weight-forward lines marketed under such titles as "Bug Taper," "Salt Water Taper," "Rocket Taper." These differences refer to how fast they taper, and that can be important for different uses. For instance, the regular Cortland weight forward is called the Rocket Taper. It gets into the body in about 12 feet. Cortland's Bug Taper fills out in a rapid 6 feet. My comments about the relative lack of difference in presentation between DT's and WF's referred to the regular weight-forward line, not to the zippy ones for specialized use, which should be kept in their useful places and stations.

MODERN NYLON LINES TO SCALE

(top) Level

(center) Double taper, 90 feet

(bottom) Weight forward, 35 yards

I would very firmly recommend that you never skimp on lines, despite price. Skimp on rods, reels, flies, cars, lovers and whatever, but don't be cheap on your only connection with your fly. Over the past few years the only really acceptable lines have been the Scientific Angler Supremes and the Cortland 444's. None of the others seem to float well, shoot smoothly through the guides or last an acceptable length of time. There are some that do one or two of these things, but only the big two do them all well. In the past there have been some other good lines, like Newton and Ashaway, but they appear and disappear and are hard to find. Avoid the lesser Cortland lines and the Air Cell Scientifics also. The top products, like the 444's and Supremes, are worth the extra money. I personally prefer the 444's over everything else on the market, but others stick with Scientifics, which were the first of the good lines. Both companies will stand behind their products, replacing them when necessary, and are, as they say of pollution-control technology, "the current state of the art." Cheaper lines are always grief.

P.S.: As you may have noticed, I have hardly mentioned level lines. This is not an accident. Despite the lingering contention of some outdoor writers (who should, but evidently don't, know better), level lines are joyless to have, except maybe an emergency one in your vest. Tapered lines are probably the most important single development in modern fly-fishing. Except for short casts, level lines do not transmit energy evenly. If money forces you to choose between a top-quality level line and a third-quality tapered one and you have any hesitation in choosing, you shouldn't have spent your money on this book. This advice goes triple for beginners— starting out with a level line would be enough to encourage you to resort to dynamite.

FLY LINE WEIGHTS

Line number	Weight (grains/30')	Tolerance in grains plus or minus
1	60	6
2	80	6
3	100	6
4	120	6
5	140	6
6	160	8
7	185	8
8	210	8
9	240	10
10	280	10
11	330	12
12	380	12

16

Leaders

There isn't a great deal that has to be said about leaders these days. If this were being written in 1960, there would have to be warnings, both implicit and explicit, about the semilevel, usually limp nylon scraps being palmed off in many quarters as tapered leaders.

But since then there has been driven home so emphatically the importance of having a fat butt, a balanced taper and a nylon connection between your line and fly that is at least somewhat stiff that almost everyone, companies included, have acknowledged the necessity of these things. Hallelujah!

The problems of the past with skinny, not very functional leaders seem to have arisen, like so many other technical fishing difficulties, during the period of transition from natural substances, i.e., silkworm gut, to the various nylon compounds which own the market today. Gut material, of which the best came from Spain, was much stiffer than the early nylon, which generally had all the spunk of 2-pound monofilament spinning line. There was little consideration given to whether the early synthetic leaders were made up hard or soft. The limp stuff was cheaper to make and easier to knot, so it was widely used.

Even though gut had to be presoaked, preferably in a glycerin solution, before it would perform correctly, had to be dried off in felt after use and could rot fairly easily, it surely did a swell job of turning a fly over, probably better than any substitute yet constructed. Some of the more devoted classicists, like Leonard Wright, still prefer gut for dry-fly fishing, but it is just about impossible to find and requires a strong devotion to purity. Good gut was never cheap either. I once picked up for sentimental reasons a batch of "Ray Bergman" gut leaders, probably from the 1940's. Named after the famed trout fisherman, these leaders cost $1.20 then, in a period when lines weren't too much more.

Sophisticated anglers forced the manufacturers to accept a few basic truths, now held to be almost self-evident. Hard nylon turns over better than soft, and the butt end of your leader should be about ⅔ to ¾ as thick as the end of your line. These factors are essential to maintain the power equation between your line and your leader, and that is what turns your fly over smartly. Of course up to a certain point it is possible to overcome an ill-conceived, limp leader by imparting more "energy" to your cast, but it is far simpler to start off with a decent leader. If your fly line ends at .030 and your leader has a maximum thickness of .012, as some shoddier ones do, there is a major loss of energy at this junction. In general the heavier the fly line the heavier your leader butt should be. This is a most important consideration.

However, this doesn't mean that you have to use only expensive dollar leaders. Begin each season by tying on a piece of butt material such as that made by Maxima or Orvis, or any of the European nylons, to equalize the difference between cheap and expensive leaders, at least to some extent. For a No. 6 line I use butt diameters of .021 or .024, though the latter may be a bit excessive. If you nail-knot or, even better, needle-knot 18 to 24 inches of this material onto the end of your line, it will usually last through the season, and will allow you to buy and use a succession of less expensive leaders, not known for their endings, by attaching them to the butt material. This will usually make the total taper okay.

This isn't necessary with the more elegant leaders, such as knotted Orvis and Cortland, because their ends are very thick already, fat enough to be tied on directly to your line. If the end of the store-bought leader is as thick as the butt material which you tied on, or thicker, the transmission of power will bog down at the junction of the two.

The longer the leader the more important these considerations of power transmission become. If your casting skills are adequate and you have tied on a section of heavy butt material and are using any acceptable commercial leader, there should be no turnover problems with leaders of 9 feet or less, taking for granted that you're not fishing in a hurricane. But if you are tying leader and line together with anything other than a nail or needle knot, you're asking for trouble, no matter how high the quality of your leader. There are still far too many anglers using little loops and other such tomfoolery at the end of their line.

If you can't turn your fly over and you've taken the aforementioned proper precautions, it's time to look at your tippet. For some anglers, especially the midge specialists, the advantages of stiffer nylon tippets don't hold. Their logic is that the softer nylons hold 20's and the like in the surface film better, allowing the fly to drift more naturally. They use the firmer stuff for all but the tippet, however. There are still many brands of tippet materials that simply aren't very good. They are relics from the bad old days of synthetic leaders. Stick if possible to the same material that your favored leaders are made from or else with good stuff like Orvis or Maxima.

This is especially true the lighter you get. The better brands of European-type nylons have a very high strength ratio for their diameter. Some of the wispy, cheaper 5X nylon I've seen is equal to the diameter of the better 7X nylon. The price difference isn't major, so go with the best. In 1975 the American market was hit with a number of expensive—75¢, $1.25—spool tippet materials from Europe. Cortland, which hit the angling public with its import, first took over much of the sales with this very fine tippet stuff, incredibly supple and strong for its diameter. These newcomers threatened to take over the market or at least that part of it peopled by knowledgeable anglers.

It is rough and awkward to turn over a big fly with a light tippet. There are no really hard and fast rules for tippet choice except the old-timer Rule of Fours passed on to us from angling antiquity. Roughly this rule says that your tippet size multiplied by 4 is about what size fly you can comfortably fish with. Even though it was thought of in the days of gut, it still holds generally true today.

A demonstration:

A 4X tippet multiplied by 4 is 16, which—plus or minus a size—is the fly you can use in a balanced delivery. A 2X tippet can handle a No. 8 fly, plus or minus a size. It isn't exact but enables the beginner at least to make a modicum of sense, regardless of where fishing. Refinement comes from experience.

There are many theories of leader design, what tapers should

BLOOD KNOT

Blood knot dropper, for attaching second fly

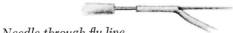

Blood knot, connecting knot for nylon leader

NEEDLE KNOT

Needle through fly line

Leader butt through fly line

Completed needle knot, best method for attaching leader butt to fly line

be used and what designs work best under what circumstances, and some are very elaborate. Most well-thought-out ones work quite well. Jack Schweigert of Roscommon, Michigan, an awesome character from my apprentice fishing days, tied fabulous double-tapered and weight-forward leaders balanced in many ways like fly lines. His 15-foot double-tapered leaders made from hard nylon back in the 60's were fine and enjoyable to use, costing over a

Nylon tippet spools

dollar apiece when most commercial leaders were fifty cents or less. But these days, though I have a fondness for the Cortland Twin Tips and Orvis's knotted, I don't worry too much about my leader anymore as long as I trust the quality of the nylon.

One thing to check out, if possible, is the vintage of the leader. Nylon can age terribly, especially in contact with the sun, and often a leader a few years old isn't worth much at all. Schweigert was the only leader tier who ever dated his creations. He wouldn't sell them after they had sat around two seasons except as half-priced bargains, and with each purchase he would always offer a stern lecture on the risks involved with aged nylon, a lesson I have yet to forget. I haven't noticed any other firms rushing to follow his lead in dating material, and some of the leaders I've seen in shops appear to have been fossilized there.

When synthetics were terrible, there used to be continuous efforts to prove that knotted leaders were superior to the smooth, continuous tapered ones. The general line of argument went that the knotted ones were better because the knots acted as energy transformers and transmitted motion better. This is undoubtedly true, but the quality of the knotless ones has improved immeasurably recently, and for 9-footers or under I don't believe there is much difference between the more expensive knotted and the smooth.

Except when fishing a whole sinking line I don't use a leader under 9 feet. For this deep-water stuff I will drop reluctantly down to 7½ feet. But I never use a shorter leader than that or, heaven forbid, a level one, as some superb anglers I know will do. I'm not good enough to give up what technological advantages I have. In the first flush of spring discoloration I start off with a 9-foot knotless El Cheapo attached to 18 inches of butt material, and by the time dry-fly fishing is peaking in August, I have graduated to a 10- to 12-foot leader attached to the butt. In some ways my outsized leaders are a psychological crutch. They make me feel much more confident of pulling a fast one on a trout, and confidence is a crucial element of angling.

A longer-than-normal but balanced leader can also be a minor compensation for, shall we say gently, a slightly below-par approach. But don't expect to build your angling strategy around long leaders! You never want to spook a rising fish by "lining" it, and you have a tad more leeway in topping your quarry with a 12-foot leader than with a 9-foot one, but only if both are straight. An old Post Creek saying is that a perfectly turned-over 7½-foot leader is far better than a 12-footer that falls in a heap on the water.

Another one of those loose-fitting generalizations: the longer your cast, the longer the leader you can handle easily. On the big rivers where 50-foot casts are a usual occurrence, a 15-foot balanced leader can be no problem, but on a mountain creek where your entire cast averages no more than 15 feet, you wouldn't dream of trying a 15-foot leader.

There are getting to be some specialized leaders available, many of which are for saltwater angling. They are often very intricate and quite expensive, with outfits like Orvis selling them for those seeking world records. The intricate leaders are available in each of the pound test brackets approved by the groups that regulate such goings-on, with peculiar knots and connections, like the Bimini Twist and the surgeon's knot. They will also, at times, have metal tippets to ward off the toothiness of barracuda and other semireptiles.

As the price of leaders has rapidly risen, so has interest in rolling out your own. Many people have discovered that tying knotted leaders together with blood knots from the kits on the market is a simple matter and kick themselves in their own thick butts for having spent scads of dollars for years on commercial leaders before discovering this simple fact. These kits, of which Orvis and Maxima are the most deservedly popular, come with elaborate directions for varieties of tapers. The kits last forever, because

159

each spool can be individually replaced as you run out, and they cost under $10. It's a good idea to chip in for a kit with angling chums, since one is more than any single angler needs.

Sometimes these kits can help you solve special angling problems. For example, there are a number of spring-creek-like sloughs in this area of Montana. These ponds and streams running into the Clark Fork and other rivers don't have many trout, but they have a few nice ones lurking around in the heavy vegetation. Like spring-creek fish everywhere, these slough trout prefer insects as the prime item of their diets, especially small insects. It is difficult to approach them in the clear shallow water, and there will often be only a 1-foot opening in the weeds to spot and cast to a rising fish. With a No. 18 to No. 20 fly on the end of a normal 10- to 12-foot 7X leader, this is about impossible. But one of the tactics of some of the home tiers is to make up a 6-foot leader out of 7X. The line rests on the vegetation of lily pads, and the fly can be accurately placed on the little opening.

Occasions for ingenuity with leaders may be rare, but they can easily be the sort of imaginative high point that makes the sport what it is.

17

Flies and Fly Tying

I

If rods and reels are the body of tackle, then flies have to be its poetic soul. They are the embodiment of an historically derived aesthetic, unique to any sport, the manifestations of theories of fishing and a window onto the trading tradition of the nations where they were made.

People far removed from fly-fishing have become totally enamored of flies; their colors, balance and design. Flytiers and collectors are often from the ranks of the nonfishing. The first time a traditional salmon pattern is seen, a different sense of functional beauty is understood, for flies are a balance of the utilitarian and the lovely. They are strict and deadly objects with a basic use value—like the blending of shapes on a venomous snake. But their appeal transcends even something as encompassing as fly-fishing. They have a lure unto themselves.

They also tell us a great deal about the state of the fishing art. Trace flies through history and you'll see how tackle development, from the early "pole" days of Juliana Berners to our present times, has allowed us to imitate with varying degrees of subtlety an ever-increasing range of fish foods. With crude tackle the fisherman could only dap his fly upon the water rather than cast it out to an exact spot. The only things that could be successfully produced from the elementary combinations of fur and feathers on those crude hooks were rough imitations of insects that came out in great numbers, blinding the fish to subtlety. This was the limitation through the nineteenth century. With cane rods and silk tapered lines that allowed casting, restrictions began slowly to dissolve. The colorful generalized wet-fly and near-surface patterns, with vague resemblances to real insects, began to be replaced by more exact imitations.

It's difficult for the late-twentieth-century angler to understand how the wily trout that today must be ingratiatingly fawned after with the most delicate equipment could have been fooled by the gross flies of earlier centuries, especially in such "laboratories" as the English chalk streams. But they and many other species were tricked for hundreds of years by patterns and combinations that we would sneer at or look on as anachronisms. A nineteenth-century bass fly, with its giant wings, is a shock to our sensitivities and a blow to our egos.

Until quite recently the tiny dries, as well as the mammoth patterns like muddlers and blondes, would have been unusable. We needed first to develop delicate tippets and lines to handle the midge flies gently, and we needed weighty shooting lines to heave out the big muddlers. All this took time. Once we could only suggest or duplicate a few insects; now we have in our fly boxes kissable cousins to minnows, mice, shrimp, bats, eels, frogs and all sorts of beasts. Yet we take this for granted. Try to make it through a season with only a few crude beginners' patterns and see how much we really have today, and be thankful. The commercial tiers certainly are!

Aside from these advances in tackle, the increasing of trade horizons gave us more possibilities for our fly patterns. You could chart the opening of the various Oriental and African trade ports by the changes in flies, especially salmon flies, which in those days used so much more variety of material than trout patterns. As the British businessmen traveled the high seas, backed by the Royal Navy in case of trouble, the anglers back on the home front weren't forgotten. Imagine the expression on the face of the first English angler to see the skin of an Amherst or golden pheasant or a jungle-cock neck. He must have realized the potential immediately.

The really ornate classic salmon patterns of the nineteenth century, when the tier's art reached its apex, could contain intricate mixtures of the feathers of ten or more exotic birds from three or four continents. The development of these patterns, which would cost a few dollars apiece today if duplicable at all, marked the high point of this angling "imperialism." Now, interestingly enough,

Muddler Minnow, favored Western streamer

Platinum Blonde, ocean fly popularized by Joe Brooks, used in big rivers

as the sun sets on the British Empire, the plebeian-hair-winged patterns developed for use by North Americans have become popular over there. Yesterday's rare feathers are no longer available. The chickens have come home to roost.

Other countries have cut off much of our free-lunching on the world's resources, justifiably annoyed at the flagrant ways we former imperialists have destroyed their natural riches. From now on we will either make do with what we find in our own countries or pay a high price.

The problem at hand, however, is to make some sense of the thousands of patterns of flies now available. There are a few basic things that one should be aware of, especially in the buying of trout flies. More attention, both in theory and practice, has been lavished on flies for trout and salmon than for bass, steelhead, saltwater species and the like, for which patterns, while important, are not as crucial as for trout. If you're using top-quality trout flies, custom-tied in the U.S., the expense can really mount up. The prices of feathery concoctions rose even faster than most other prices during the 1970's. During the past few years some of the larger fly brokers in this country started having flies tied in Third World countries to avoid American labor costs. Even though our tiers are paid meager amounts for their straining work (usually $2 to $3 per dozen for flies that are individually retailed for the staggering markup of $8 to $9 per dozen), the dealers want higher profits. What the American-trained Third World tiers get must be minuscule. Good flies cost as much as $1 and usually not less than 75¢ apiece. Using light tippets that break easily can make the expense really mount up. One 1975 fancy catalog listed some tiny No. 18 and No. 20 midges at 85¢, with the warning that they suffer a casualty rate of a couple an hour.

Traditionally, patterns have been broken down into the subgroupings of imitators, suggestors and attractors, but trout don't read the magazines. It doesn't matter to them that a No. 16 Hendrickson supposedly duplicates a particular hatching mayfly, or that a White Wulff suggests a hatching white miller. Despite the most persuasive claims, all flies are really suggestors.

In some ways, fly-fishing is an analytic pursuit. That is, some angling authorities are endlessly trying to categorize trout foods with a higher and higher degree of specialization. The general drift of their argument is that every major dietary preference of the various salmons can be objectively understood and, at least theoretically, duplicated. This reasoning has gotten energetic beginners into a morass of purchases from which there is small chance of escape. The charts and books which stress imitative patterns as the end-all of trout fishing follow this theory, which is simply not true—at least in my experience. Hatch matching is more an idea than a reality.

Adams, traditional dry fly originated in Michigan

The earliest fly patterns all suggested various fish foods as well as the materials of the day would allow. With the twentieth century's technological advances, the suggestors have tried to become imitators. Precise patterns are used for every emerging insect, like a natural chess game; for each move a countermove. Bird's salmon fly is used when the giant stone fly is upon Western waters and Cahills when the Cahills are out in force. At other times we are supposed to use patterns such as the various caddis flies. Out of desperation, when nothing happens, we are supposed to attack our quarry with attractors—those large bright-colored things like the Wulffs and Coachmen. It is accepted but not spoken that anglers and their flies go through stages of development; from the attractors to the suggestors to the heavenly perfection of fishing with imitators. (Though angling fashions today are generally cool toward attractors, favoring a more and more—*mm*—pseudoscientific approach to our sport, like the NFL's scientific offenses and defenses . . . imitation of duns and then paraduns and then stillborn paraduns—*hrmpp!*)

Actually the beginner would do best with a few tried-and-true suggestor patterns and no exact imitations. It really is a dubious dream to try to imitate any hatching insect exactly. Under various light and water conditions patterns take on various characteristics to trout. It would take an almost infinite number of patterns to duplicate exactly any one hatching form in the direct light of noon, the diffused light of evening and the reflected morning sun. Flies appear very different to fish on cloudy days, on cloudless days and on days that are combinations of the two. This is true for near-surface nymphs as well as dries.

Suggestor patterns, on the other hand, that are the same general size, color and shape of a group of insects can give fish the idea that what they're gazing at is the real McCoy during most of the day. A fly more closely approximating the actual insect can do this only for a little while on a given day and might look like a Studebaker the rest of the time. Buying suggestors is a real saving, since it doesn't require as many patterns as the exact-imitation route. A few basic patterns will suffice for just about the entire season. This isn't to argue that the longtime veteran angler should throw out his exact-imitation collection built up through the years. The beginner, however, should consider the initial investment required to start out with dozens of imitations at a buck apiece. It can equal the price of a decent rod very quickly and serve no important function.

If hatch matching was really the only right way, it would be impossible to account for the success of the attractor patterns and the more outlandish suggestors. Despite the claims of some outdoor writers, the Royal Coachman is an attractor fly, as is the Wooly Worm. All deerhair flies should go in the category of suggestors. Fish take these patterns with great regularity, except for certain moments during certain hatches when they become very selective.

Another strike against the theory of exact imitation is the utter failure of the very exact rubber-and-plastic insect imitations. Except for bass, which will take rubber worms, fish seem to prefer the translucence of bodies and wings constructed from organic sources. They respond to light diffused through these substances rather than something that is seemingly exact in every way but synthetic. It indicates that there has to be a compromise between material, detail and form for overall success.

If you don't believe that your approach is more important than exact imitation, try fishing with an Adam, Quill Gordon or other general patterns all season long. You won't notice much difference in your total catch at the end of the year. The beginner especially should be more concerned with presentation and reading the water than with the perfection of the fly.

All the same, for some people the choice of fly patterns is a serious concern, not meant to be joked about.

Some years back, Preston Jennings, author of *A Book of Trout Flies* and an important figure in pre-Schwiebert hatch matching, was holding forth on the imitation of minnows. A group of people at a lodge on Pennsylvania's Brodhead River listened intently as he described in intricate detail how to duplicate various trout fodders exactly.

Ed Zern, the talented *Field and Stream* columnist, was a young angling iconoclast then. He listened to the convolutions of Jennings's logic until his patience ran out, then interrupted, saying approximately, "I don't believe you can possibly tie a streamer pattern that I can't catch a fish with. Furthermore I'll bet you anything you like that I can use any color combination to fool a trout."

Jennings stormed out of the gathering, and for the rest of his years would never even acknowledge Zern's existence.

Of course what Zern said was true, even for the educated

Western mayfly

Brodhead fish, but some anglers are so into systems of exact imitation that they won't admit their structures have only an inner logical consistency.

On the other hand, when Dick Eggert and I first fished with Robert Traver, Dick got very frustrated by Traver's insistence on refusing to identify patterns by their correct names. Dick was going through his "impressed by the experts" stage and thought that he would be enlightened that day by fishing Michigan's Upper Peninsula with Traver. However, Traver would only refer to the flies he thought should be used as, "that little brown one" or "the pretty black thing." Dick has since outgrown his impatience.

There are a number of semimystical, semitried-and-true practices that generalize on how to choose flies. For some they work and for some they don't, but they are worth listing anyway, if only for amusement.

The major consideration in fooling trout with a fly is size. Trout are more aware of this than anything else. Next comes the form of the offering. If the natural has big wings and a tiny body, your choice should have the same outline. The last probable concern for a trout when looking at a pseudodinner is color. Size, form and color in that order. If trout are nipping your fly without taking or are ignoring one that looks in most respects like the natural, drop down a size. That sometimes works. It can get costly, but once in a while it pays to trim the body of a refused offering, and at other times nothing will do except a whole different color. If there were a simple solution to these questions, there wouldn't be thousands of books and as many divergent opinions. Don't let any self-anointed expert, myself included, convince ' you otherwise. Fish are the final arbiters of all fishing techniques—not glib humans. Despite the outpourings of those outdoor writers for whom each trip is a method for personal triumph over their quarry, vindicating their intelligence and savvy, we shall continue to get skunked at least from time to time. Anyone claiming otherwise is merely a liar.

There have been innumerable attempts in the history of angling to codify the sport, to make it a simple surefire thing, by codifying the dietary habits of fish. Thank goodness they have all failed.

Though a large amount of regionalism is involved in fly selection, of course, there are a few suggestor patterns that could get you through in a pinch just about anywhere you'll find yourself. When I mention some of these flies, you are going to snap back with, "They ain't suggestors, they're exact imitations of the giant moose hatch which occurs on Gitchegummee Creek in my backyard every other Thursday in July."

True, no doubt, but what is an imitation in one area may be a suggestor in another, hence the more than adequate performance of the Hendrickson in many Montana streams.

Anyway, here are the few basic suggestors I would start with: Adams Nos. 16 to 20, Gray Wulffs Nos. 12 to 16, Irresistibles or Humpies Nos. 14 to 16, Muddler Minnows Nos. 10 to 14 (not weighted), Rio Grande King trude Nos. 12 to 14 and light Cahill Nos. 16 to 20.

Here's a list of should's and should-not's about flies.

1. They should be balanced. The wings should be at proper angles from each other and the whole fly should be symmetrical.

2. The head should be tight, even and small. Rube Cross, the best classical tier this country ever produced, put no noticeable heads on his flies. Big bulky heads are always a bad sign.

3. The hackles on a dry fly should be stiff. Compare it to a wet fly. There should be a big difference.

4. The body should be tight all the way through. Nothing loose anywhere.

5. On hair flies, the bodies and wings should be evenly trimmed. No assorted hairs coming out in strange places.

6. Tinsel and other metal should be firmly tied in at both ends.

7. Hackles should be made from two feathers rather than one.

JOE'S HOPPER

(left) Correct

(right) Split turkey wing

8. Beware of clipped hackles and wings—a sure sign of bad materials.

9. The pattern should be exact. No virtuoso performances with your money unless there is a compelling reason for it.

10. The fly should be an organic whole, completely integrated, with nothing strange anywhere.

These characteristics should hold whether it is a trout fly, bass fly or saltwater bombast. Neatness, not originality, counts in flies. For bass fishing, however, I much prefer the cork bugs over the hair-bodied ones. They last longer and can be "chugged" across the surface effectively. Hair frogs and the like can cost $2 each, while cork ones are usually about half that price.

For saltwater flies, check out the hooks. If they aren't rust-proof, there can be problems. In general, hooks should be reasonably balanced to the purpose of the fly. Floaters should have light hooks and sinkers as heavy as practical. Ask the dealer what hooks

ADAMS

(left) Correct

(right) Tail pointing down, body not tapered properly, hackle too long, wings too large and too far forward, big bulky head

169

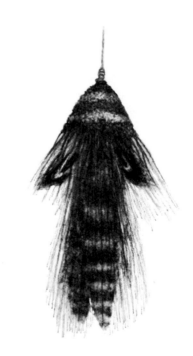

Whitlock Sculpin as tied by Dave Newkirk

his creations are tied on. With soaring prices, some tiers are cutting corners, and nothing less than Mustads will do. Many cheap hooks will snap under strain just like your temper.

Seen the light? Going to tie your own masterpieces? Your troubles aren't over yet. You will have to undergo the ordeal or pleasure of buying the supplies, not to mention learning how to tie.

Once again, don't skimp on materials. Less of the good stuff is better than more of the bad. You can always upgrade your supplies while tying a few decent patterns at the same time. If you have poor-quality materials you can only tie a lot of shoddy patterns.

There are few real shortcuts or alternatives to experience in buying materials. Many years of background are required to detect quality in the variety of furs, feathers and assorted substances now on the market. Buy from a specialty or custom shop if at all possible. Getting your basics from a store that has bought its material prepackaged from who knows where doesn't make sense. These people usually don't know much about what they are selling, and in something as crucial as fly material, you can waste tying hours for naught. Even a beginner can tie some at least adequate flies, like deerhair caddis, with good materials. It isn't terribly difficult, especially if you can find someone knowledgeable in the craft to look them over with you. That is one of the pleasures of their knowledge—helping their lessers out! Return privileges on materials are important, so demand them. Most reputable firms guarantee their stuff, anyway. In the rush of sorting out necks or whatevers, even the most conscientious dealer can make an oversight.

HACKLE

Your major expense in tying material is hackle, the necks of elderly chickens used in wets, dries and nymphs—almost everything, actually. Dry-fly necks, which float your fly and range in price from $3 to $25, come from tough old roosters. Stiffness is a prime virtue, since the hackle has to support the fly, and accordingly the dry-fly necks are the most valuable. Many soft, wet-fly necks are produced for each prime-quality dry-fly neck that ends up on a flytier's bench.

Look for a neck with the largest amount of individual feathers in the size you most often tie or plan to tie. An experienced eye can break the feathers on a given neck into 10's, 14's and so on very quickly. Some anglers, trying to be impressive, get into the habit of searching for necks with the most No. 18 or smaller feathers, though most people use this size fly rarely.

The important qualities of a neck, aside from size and stiffness, are the length of the feathers, the sheen they have and the webbing (the less the better). They should also have the thinnest rib or quill possible. Thick quills are hard to handle while tying.

As for colors, most of the prime grizzly in the world comes from the United States. The recent surge of interest in tying has made it financially worthwhile for some poultry farmers to raise roosters for their necks. Since older birds have the best hackle, five years is considered prime. They aren't much good for the table, maybe, but who ever got $20 for a fryer? A few companies are now offering supergrade grizzly necks priced at $25 or more, and the birds are raised like prize poodles. I hate to say it, but they are worth the pampering. Grizzly is a very useful neck, and the supers have three to four times more usable feathers, which are at least one-third longer than on a neck that costs half the price. These necks also have a good distribution of individual feather sizes, so that one neck will meet all your grizzly tying needs. Actually, there are enough feathers on them to make it worth your going into partnership with a friend to buy one. Unless you go into commercial tying, the two of you won't use it up for several years.

For the other neck colors, you will have to make do with imports. In the old days, most of the browns, blacks, whites, natural blue dun and variations came from China. But when that country stopped existing for the State Department in 1948, we anglers had to depend on India and the Philippines for our supply. Now we are getting some from the People's Republic again.

The Chinese necks are usually high quality, but they don't have as many tiny feathers (for flies No. 16 to No. 28) as the Indian necks. The Indian ones also have a more uniform size distribution and the feathers are longer, with less webbing. The Philippine necks are best for bigger flies. Their feathers are long, with stiff ribs.

Each neck color has different characteristics. For instance, both white and black necks are almost always soft, and decent-quality dry-fly ones are rare. Brown necks, on the other hand, tend to be stiff and a good buy.

Another possible value are the so-called Laos Mix or Nairobi variants—a multicolored neck. They have some stiff white feathers mixed in with the dominating brown ones, which are very good for dry flies—a bonus deal, especially nice since they are usually priced low because of a lack of commercial interest. The much-vaunted blue duns, the most desirable of all necks for some patterns, are almost all coming from China and are usually not so great. They are more wet-fly quality than dry and resemble a black neck more than a blue. A few years back, blue dun necks were as rare as the Holy Grail and probably sought after with more interest, bringing as much as $100 when available.

A general tip for the hackle buyer is not to overlook the potential of saddle hackles. They are much, much cheaper than a comparable neck in colors like grizzly and work quite well for flies No. 12 and smaller. Most tiers overlook these body feathers, but they can save you money.

HAIR

Hair for spinners should be long and large and free of under-fur and come from a mule or white-tailed deer.

For wings and tails, it should be short, thick and well barred to control flaring. The best hair for this tying comes from the West Coast blacktail.

Be sure the hair is consistent in color. A black should be black and not blue, something simple but often overlooked.

Elk hair, which has a variety of applications in tying, should be straight. It can run from white to black and in between, so check it out.

TURKEY

Buy some of the mottled turkey used for muddlers and other similar flies. The mottled turkey has been replaced by poultry growers with white birds and will probably be unobtainable in a few years, so hoard a dollar's worth.

PEACOCK

Good iridescent green peacock has heavy herl that is relatively wide. In stripping peacock eyes for such beauties as the Quill

173

Gordon, you'll want as large an eye as possible. The back of the eye should be gray and not brown for this sort of use.

ANGORA

For many body applications, spun angora wool makes a fine and inexpensive substitute for the tedious work of dubbing fur, and few fish went far enough in school to detect the difference. The angora is available in a great range of colors already wound on cards. Polypropylene, which has become popular recently, is held in some disfavor by purists because it is unnatural. They may be correct in a spiritual sense, but it sure is another tying time-saver. At least in the beginning, go with angora.

HOOKS

Hooks have to be Mustads, alas. I've always favored the English brands, like Seeley and Allcock, but astronomical costs and other considerations in today's not-so-merry England have drastically curtailed, if not eliminated, their availability. Mustads are going up as well, but don't be cheap on hooks. Use dry-fly hooks for dries and wet-fly hooks for wets, too. Everything has its place. If you are a millionaire, you might consider salmon fly hooks for your nymphs and wets. At a nickel-plus each they run into money, but are elegant and heavy.

DUCK FEATHERS

Use more teal, a neglected duck, over mallard for smaller wings. Teal is very good for the no-hackle flies of Swisher-Richards fame.

VISES AND TOOLS

Go with quality, I guess. Thompson, which for years have made the best vises available, have been going upward in cost and, it must be interjected, down in quality. They are probably still the best general ones around, though. The new Orvis vise, for—wow—$37.50 looks much hardier than any other vise around. I once had a vise that was made by a Detroit automotive engineer for his personal use in a Ford Motor Company machine shop. It

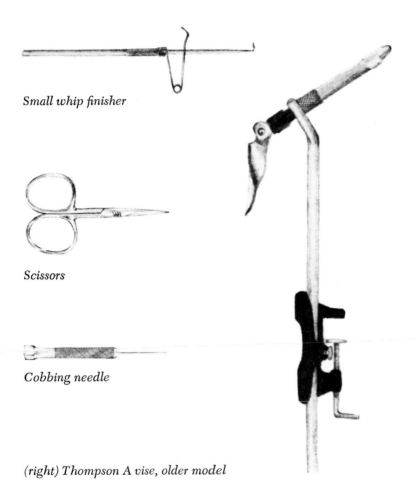

Small whip finisher

Scissors

Cobbing needle

(right) Thompson A vise, older model

was head and shoulders above any other vise I've ever seen, so you might make your own. I'm definitely not an engineer, so I'll leave it to you.

Doctor's tools, such as scissors, clamps and forceps, make fine fly-tying accessories and are better than most commercial tools. At the price of medical care in this society, you should get the doctor to throw something in.

Some of the commercial fly-tying tools are usable, but check out workmanship carefully. By the way, test out hackle pliers before buying. Some of them have the nasty habit of biting off more feathers than they should chew.

175

Hackle pliers

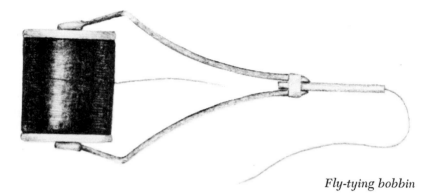

Fly-tying bobbin

THREADS

The beginner can get by with only two kinds of thread, such as 6/0 prewaxed Danville and 3/0 Monocord, waxed or unwaxed at your pleasure. Nymo is a great thread if you can find some. The two flat threads can take care of both your little and big flies, the best of all possible tying worlds.

One thing must be added about materials in general. The brighter and gaudier the stuff is the less it usually has to offer. The prepackaged racks are usually full of blue squirrel tail and chartreuse necks—both of very dubious usefulness. For inland trout fishing, stay with the somber colors as befits a serious, undaunted piscator. The garish colors are okay for steelhead, especially if fluorescent, and some untutored saltwater fish, but not for trout. Experimentation is definitely the backbone of tying, but get the basics down in basic colors before proceeding on your inventive own. You gotta walk before you can run.

P.S. Try a local taxidermist for assorted bits and pieces of fur and feathers.

18

Odds and Ends

There is a large amount of leeway in our recreational indulgences. Almost every angler I've met is an impulse buyer, searching for the Holy Gadget and accumulating piles of things of dubious utility along the trail.

The worst offenders are usually big-city and suburb dwellers, trapped in a ritualized existence that gives little room to breathe deep. The most tackle-conscious people are not Montana anglers (admittedly, there are a few major exceptions), who can fish all the time, but the subterraneans of New York's canyons, who nurture their fishing dreams long and hard.

Ed Zern warned me a few years ago, when the big bucks of city life became somewhat alluring, about its psychic perils. He simply detailed his daily lunchtime odysseys through Abercrombie & Fitch, the Park Place William Mills shop, now no longer in business, and the sports shelves of several bookstores. This was how he mentally escaped the rigors of an advertising agency. Consuming and buying can become a substitute for doing.

Zern scared me so badly that I moved to Montana as soon as possible, not passing Go and not collecting $200, where I have lived in poverty surrounded by fishing tackle ever since. There may not be a direct causal relationship between the dissatisfaction we feel in our lives and the amount of impulse buying we engage in, but there is at least some connection. We all seem to believe subconsciously that buying things will make us happier.

Though the cliché in this society is the woman buying a new hat or dress to combat depression, the reality includes her husband buying a new fishing vest or reel when feeling morose. That's about the only way we are allowed to react to our sadness—with things. Women are no more subject to these idiosyncrasies than men, only the objects vary.

I've begun this discussion of something as lighthearted as assorted accessories on a sullen note because of the dangers inherent in any discussion of fishing paraphernalia. There are almost an infinite number of things to splurge on and many of us will do just that. An encyclopedia could be written on fishing gadgets alone. They can be a minor accessory before the fact of bankruptcy as well. This chapter will be fairly crisp, limiting indulgences as much as possible, but it will probably be like trying to hold back the tide. I don't want to contribute to anyone's angling delinquency, so this disclaimer was mandatory. Now you're on your own.

FLY BOXES

I can feel my pledge dissolving already. Fly containers are neat things, especially those made in England or the kind that William Mills used to sell.

It always seems that our changing angling values, new fashions in flies and our ever-increasing burden of patterns make it obligatory to own one, then another, then another additional box. If an angel mysteriously appeared on the stream and handed us three patterns that would catch fish anywhere, anytime, we would buy another box and put the Eternal Trio in it, along with our thousands of other patterns.

A history of fly-fishing could be roughly outlined from fly boxes, which, incidentally, are now a separate subcategory among tackle collectors. In the nineteenth century, before the ascendancy of surface lures, flies were transported in thick leather wallets with felt pages that kept and dried the snelled wets. As many as a dozen bulging pages held the gentleman's fur-and-feather combinations together. These fly books had side compartments for gut leaders and points with felt pads to keep them moist before use.

The dry fly brought major changes. The all-important stiffer hackle, which kept the fly on top of things, had to be protected. The first compartmentalized dry-fly boxes were usually like the modern Common Sense boxes, having a box for dry flies and also the wallet-type arrangement with felt leaves for wets. There are

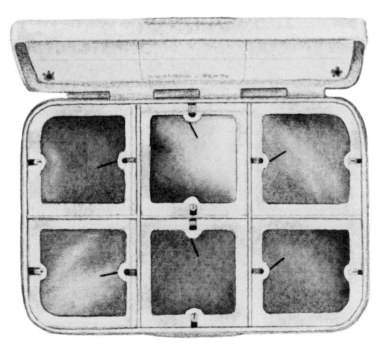

Six-compartment Wheatley dry-fly box

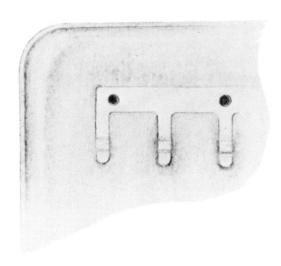

Section of Perrine salmon-fly box

some fine Common Sense kits available at very reasonable prices, by the way, that will accommodate all your flies.

Looking over early catalogs is an appetite-whetting experience for the tackle freak. They show a staggering variety of styles and designs of fly boxes, some of which would probably cost $100 to duplicate today. In almost all tackle groupings there was a far better selection fifty years ago. The current fly-fishing renaissance, which has brought more people than ever before into the sport, has not brought about a true revival of fine tackle, except for rods. Tackle production seems generally subsumed under our corporate system of sameness. There are still a few very fine things being made, but not with the variety of, say, the 1920's.

Tackle wallets and other such holders can often be found in secondhand stores and bought for loose change, since there isn't much of a market for them. Many of these semiantiques were made of very fine quality leather. Their felt pages, usually badly worn, can be replaced by sewing in new felt. Chamois or its imitations can be placed between the felt pages for drying flies after use.

Wallets, relics these days, are actually a mistakenly neglected item. Almost none are now being made, yet they are the best home for big saltwater streamers and work very well for any wet fly or nymph. The nicest wallet I own was cut out for me by a local leatherworker according to my simple design. It shuts with a strap and buckle, is about 4 by 6 inches, has felt pages with artificial chamois and two side pockets for leaders and tippets. It cost $5 to assemble, with me sewing the felt, and would cost at least $25 if it could be purchased.

Streamer wallet, all leather

The Wheatley Company makes a nice nymph and wet-fly wallet with an assortment of niches and holders. The pages of this fly book have Wheatley's well-known clips to hold the flies in place. But the book retails for $20 or so now.

The most popular types of fly boxes are made of metal and/or plastic. There is one basic word to remember about plastic fly boxes—soft. Always get the unbreakable ones marketed under such names as Tenite and Pyra-Shell. They give you all the protection necessary and don't shatter on impact. As they age, they get darker, which is nice and quite a trick for plastic. The cheaper, hard plastic boxes, which don't claim to be unbreakable, are heavier and prone to hinge-snapping. A few years ago the soft ones, produced by the DeWitt Company, were a vanishing breed, but almost everyone is merchandising them now.

From a practical standpoint, one of the nicest containers I have ever owned was a gift from Ed Zern. The box is just perfect for dries. Made from soft plastic, it has twelve individual compartments, each with its own lid like the Wheatley metal fly boxes. Every compartment has a little plastic snap to lock it. Probably made in the 1940's, it combines the lightness and toughness of the transparents plus the safety from wind and snazziness of the Wheatleys.

Now a few words about Wheatleys—they're swell. Wheatley is a fine old English company that has been making the best metal fly boxes for a long time. Admittedly, the ones of a few decades back were more elegant and better constructed than the current models. The prices for Wheatleys have doubled and in some cases tripled over the past few years as well. My thirty-two-compartment box, with its delicate sections and tiny springs, now sells for $50-plus, and it was only a decade or so ago that a very decent rod could be acquired for that kind of money. The Wheatley dry-fly boxes can be easily jammed and are as heavy as an anvil. Still, many flycasters splurge with one or more sooner or later, because they are so admirable. The first time you gaze at a Wheatley is always an eye-popping experience. The small six-compartment box is excellent for midge dries, and the models that combine dry-fly compartments on one side with clips for nymphs and wets on the other are ideal if you just take one container out.

The Wheatley metal boxes for underwater offerings are the best on the market as well. They make many types, for everything from the biggest salmon flies to the tiniest nymphs and all manner

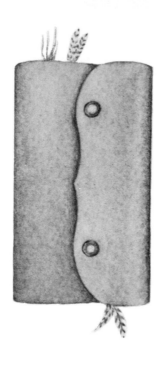
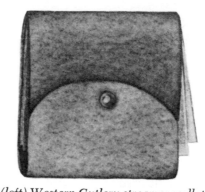

(left) Western Cutlery streamer wallet

(right) Leader wallet from 1930's

of combinations. Some models hold flies and leaders and some have metal leaves for extra carrying capability.

An interesting sidelight to the compartmentalized boxes like the Wheatleys is that they were designed for use in the south of England, where there is almost a perpetual stiff breeze. Dry-fly anglers in those turn-of-the-century days wanted boxes that wouldn't expose their whole fly collection to the vagaries of the wind every time they wanted a replacement fly. But since then, often for strictly aesthetic reasons, they have caught on around the trout world—even where there is nary a breeze.

Though Perrine boxes and the Scientific Angler fly holders are popular among anglers, few people would hesitate to switch to Wheatley if they had the option. Beware of Wheatleys around salt water, however, because they don't belong there. On a practical level, the Perrines and the like—with rows of slips or snaps for flies—work fine.

There are some lovely leather leader wallets available, but they are a decadent luxury, since most anglers nowadays carry only a couple of extra leaders. Whether fine leather is necessary to carry two flat leaders is a matter between you and your maker.

VESTS AND KIT BAGS

At long last, kit bags are beginning to make a comeback in this country. A hundred years ago, both Americans and the English favored bags for carrying tackle, though our paths have diverged in this century. The British angler held on to his usually canvas side bag and we Americans switched over to vests, but in the past few years more and more of us have begun going back to the old ways. There are two sides to this matter, and it isn't hard to build up a case either way. I don't bother and use whichever one strikes my fancy when I head out to the stream.

Tackle bags of the sort sold by Orvis and Eddie Bauer, as well as many English firms, can hold relatively bulky things like coats, lunches, wine, books and binoculars. If you start wading too deep, they can be held straight up or out. They can also be taken off easily, be switched around for comfort and be used as a makeshift pillow at naptime.

Vests, on the other hand, are very convenient. You can get to things more easily with a little foresight, and they will hold tons of things, too. The departmentalization lends itself well to the diversity of modern fly-fishing.

Whichever way you go, beware of size. Bigger things aren't always better. There is an unbeatable principle in fishing that states, in essence, that every nook and cranny of your tackle holder must be filled, without regard to weight or expense. If you have a crowded by 8-by-10-inch bag and believe for a moment that a 10-by-12-inch one would be more handy, forget it. As soon as you get the bigger bag you'll discover that you can't possibly go out again without a portable octopus degorger and harpoon gun, which will overcrowd the new bag worse than the old one.

The finest bag I've ever seen now sits on my wall. It is a large Hardy 12-by-16-incher, and when even half full it is simply much too much of a burden for comfortable fishing. In all its magnificence, it has become decoration, bringing "Oohs" and "Ahs" from admirers. On those rare ceremonial occasions when I take it out, I wind up leaving it on the bank and scurry ashore for every need.

The same is true with vests. I own a brand called, not imaginatively, The Vest. It really is an ultimate commodity, with pockets on top of pockets inside of pockets. But here again, it is a bit overloaded, especially in late season when the weather gets very warm and clambering down the cliffs in the Big Hole Canyon and other rugged big-fish hideouts is a sweaty business.

Try to be honest with yourself. How much stuff will you really be carrying and how much of that stuff do you really need? Get a vest or bag that will be adequate but not overabundant. It sometimes seems that only the very expensive vests are made well and that they have hundreds of pockets more than needed, but you can look around and find exceptions. If you carry a big load, beware of vests of thin material. They really crumple up under pressure. Also check the zippers out carefully, as they are often the manufacturing weak spot.

These days, having a vest or a kit bag custom-made usually is not much more expensive than buying one off the rack, especially if you're going in for top quality. There are lots of sewers and leatherworkers who can build you a bag or vest of your choice. Often they are nicer than those made by someone who is attempting to fit the needs of the largest number of potential customers.

Dan Bailey vest

Tackle kit bag

Vests and bags are very important to the modern angler, enveloped in gear. Have your bag or vest assembled so that it is easy to find what you want when you want it. Grasping and searching every time you need a fix of dry-fly dope is a drag. Get the bag or vest you need and learn to use it.

I don't think much of the plastic fly-fisherman's tackle boxes that are around. If you are going to be out on a boat or some other semistationary place, a kit bag still works better. Plastic boxes can be nerve-racking in such situations, always falling over or disintegrating under your nose.

In the past few years, the Mann-type metal-shelf fly boxes have again become popular. These boxes, harnessed around the neck, can hold an incredible number of flies and come equipped with leather leader pouches by Orvis and in any custom style by Richardsons. They are great for the fly-fastidious trout angler who likes to carry hundreds of patterns in varying compartments. They come with up to five shelves, with sixteen big compartments in each shelf. Some models have places to attach flotant, flashlights and sponge-rubber holders for wet flies and nymphs. For some people, they eliminate the need for either a vest or bag, though there is no room for things like lunch, raincoats or brandy.

FLOATERS AND SINKERS

Dry-fly flotants come in only a few basic types. There are the old-time wax and white gas mixes, the mucilin-based liquids and pastes and the aerosols, usually made with some sort of silicone. As a rule of thumb, I prefer the pastes or 1:10 paraffin–white gas mixtures for very large dries and muddlers. For small flies, I use either a mucilin or silicone mixture. The squeeze bottle of Seidel's compound also works very well.

I never use aerosols and believe that no angler should. These containers are a possible menace to us all because of the effect of aerosol dispensers on the earth's ozone. They are also wasteful, and anyone serious about the future of the sport shouldn't patronize fly sprays that are potentially hazardous and the antithesis of recyclable. They typify our push-button mentality. If we fishermen get away with our little wastefulness, then the next person is justified in his little aberrations and so on down that horrid line we all tread in our slightly different ways out of our slightly different necessities. They are popular, work well and are convenient, but we pay too high an environmental price to use them.

The sinking compounds for leaders and flies all seem to work okay, but I personally find little use for them. When my leader needs its surface scratched, I use soap or toothpaste or draw it through rubber. I have made dozens of leader straighteners and tension breakers from scraps of belts my leatherworker friend gives me, and some of these end pieces are very elaborately carved.

Here's how to do it. Take a 3- or 4-inch strip of leather, 1½ or 2 inches wide. On the roughest side, glue two pieces of inner tube so that they face each other when you fold the piece between your fingers. Cut a hole on each side of the crease so you can attach the little beauty to your bag or vest with a lace. By pulling a leader through the rubber, you can break the surface tension and simultaneously straighten it. These things come out pretty fancy, take only minutes to make and are nice angling "favors."

The commercial leader and fly-sinking compounds are sometimes really needed with tiny flies and tippets that have trouble piercing the water's surface tension. For some fishing situations nothing else may do, but you will usually know ahead when you'll need it.

Products like Leonard's Fly-Dry are very handy, if not vital. They work surprisingly well to rejuvenate flies that have been mouthed by fish. My regular routine is to use this white powder after having a fish on whether the fly seems to need it or not. They are real fly savers, quickly removing slime and gunk. If you're not rich and buy your flies instead of tying them, this stuff is a money saver, too.

One sentence in general about all these floating, sinking and reclaiming concoctions. Despite the toutings of producers, from a practical standpoint I don't think there is much difference between them. I know too many people who are happy with many different kinds of floaters and sinkers to believe that anything other than quirk really counts.

SPLIT-SHOT SINKERS

I use tiny sinkers much of the time, believing that usually a fly that is unweighted and sunk with a tiny piece of Pezon-Michel split shot 3 inches above it has better action than a weighted fly. I'm in love with these French minishots, ranging in size from the "giant" 1/64th ounce to God knows how tiny. They really do the job for any kind of deep angling. Since I found the splits, which most of the bigger supply houses now stock, I've quit using the wraparound lead and lead threads that used to drive me up a wall to get on a leader. The splits are perfect for sinking flies, and you just never know when you could use one. They can be a little tricky to cast, though, and you must never overload a rod with them.

KNIVES

I have a really excellent fish-cleaning knife that was made for me by Ruana, the venerable old Finnish maker who lives in Bonner, Montana. Like any good filleting knife, it has a very thin blade that is perfect for cleaning and filleting fish. With its elk-horn handle, brass guard and lanyard holder, it is another of those ultimate commodities.

But actually, for most fishing, any small pen or pocketknife will do. If you're heading for salt water, stainless knives should be your choice. The brine can do unspeakable horrors in short order to conventional metal blades. Among the nicer specifically fish-cleaning knives I've seen are the Gerber, Fin-Nor and Orvis, but there are plenty of others.

The really neat knives are the small fly-fisherman's models that used to be quite common. At one time, Case, Hardy and the Swiss Army all made such things, and they are sometimes still available if you are in the right place at the right time. I have a small Puma fly-fisherman's tool that I picked up at Abercrombie's ten years ago. It has a scissors, little blade, disgorger (just right for a minnow), hard rough edge for use as hook sharpener and a tweezer of sorts.

More than these goodies you should have, first of all, a clipper. You really can't do an adequate job of cutting leaders with either a knife blade or scissors. The clipper makes short work of something that we frantic moderns do all the time—change flies. We use clippers more than miniature disgorgers or hook straighteners.

Sometimes handy knives for fly-fishing can be picked up at pipe shops, which usually carry an assortment with neat appurtenances like scissors and tweezers. Take care of your knives; moisture has a way of hiding in them and rusting them slowly away. Keep them well oiled.

On the order of knives, get a jeweler's screwdriver. If you are spectacled and reeled, and if a screw on your reel (or glasses) starts coming loose, this tiny screwdriver can be invaluable. You can pick one up fairly reasonably.

REPAIR KIT

While on the subject of screwdrivers, if you spend lots of time fishing, you might consider a small repair kit, containing an extra tip-top, a couple of assorted guides, tape, wrapping silk and a little varnish. Such kits were sold in the 20's and 30's, but we seem to have developed more trust in technology. However, they are easy to put together. Such a kit will weigh only an ounce or so and could make all the difference, one unfortunate day.

CREELS

For those of us who still keep a fish or two, willow creels are the nicest. Some of the old ones were really lovely. It's getting hard to find good willow creels, but secondhand stores are the places to begin. The few still being made are very expensive.

The rattan ones that used to be sold by Leonard and Paul Young were small and flat and kept fish very fresh, but they couldn't be used as many Westerners used willow creels—as a fishing kit bag. They were designed to be folded up until needed.

One possibility is to make a small creel (don't be greedy) from a gunnysack. This small fabric bag will keep fish fresh, especially when some willow or similar leaves are thrown in. My kit bag has a fishnet side and I carry a small gunny bag which I use to hold the fish in the netting. It works fine. There are any number of other solutions, including canvas creels that clip on your vest and the Arctic creels that work very well. I've noticed that some catalogs no longer carry such things—giving the distinct impression that only rascals keep fish. It might be a more impressive moral stand if they ever talked about the corporations' role in destroying our fisheries.

In an absolute pinch, a small plastic bag can be used, but holes for ventilation must be cut, and some moist grass should be thrown in. For fishing from a boat, take along a cooler. That's really best.

NETS

Though Western anglers have traditionally eschewed nets, they are starting to come back into fashion, and a good thing, too. Despite Walter Mittty visions of our grace and adroitness, it is very easy to damage a fish while landing it. Nets help eliminate this danger. They aren't hard to carry, with one of those retrieving gadgets to keep them out of the way, and can be convenient. The traditional nets are the Cumminses, made in Michigan, but Joe Swaluk has been making some gorgeous ones recently for about $30. The wooden frame ones, made from hickory and walnut mixes, appeal to me aesthetically, but the Insta-Nets are very good as well and more handy. These nets fit into a holster arrangement, and their wire frames pop open when pulled.

The inexpensive aluminum nets work as well as any of the fancier ones, and they are usually much lighter. Another example of tradition versus practicality in fly-fishing.

For salt and brackish waters, avoid linen netting. Get nylon, of course.

Just make sure that your net will hold the fish you will encounter. It is a tragicomedy to try to land your lunker and to discover it won't fit into the net, or to watch it fall through the bottom.

PRIESTS

Impractical as hell, but the Hardy and Leonard priests for bonking fish on the head are nice pieces of paraphernalia which I obligingly haul around. Don't ask me why! A rock does the job as well, but rocks aren't usually made of brass and hickory and don't cost around $10.

Hardy priest, trout-sized

STONES

Carry around a small piece of Arkansas or other quality stone, preferably with a groove in it, for sharpening hooks when necessary. You can epoxy the stone to a piece of wood and attach it to the outside of your vest or bag. There may be some commercial hook-sharpening stones left, but if so, they are likely to be inconvenient to carry or not very good.

FLASHLIGHTS

Though I wouldn't want to be stranded on a desert island with just a Flex Light, they are best for the fly-fisherman. They have extra-convenient goosenecks and clips to hang them on various parts of your apparel. There are plenty of other decent, or even better-quality, lights on the market, but this one seems right for all-around fishing. Sometimes a flashlight can be a lifesaver, so don't neglect it if you plan to stay out all day. I've had much more than $6 worth of use from mine.

FORCEPS

Definitely get a pair of physician's forceps if you can. Either the curved or the straight ones are great as hook disgorgers, emergency vises and a trillion other things. The ones that the tackle houses now merchandise are okay, but the genuine article is better and can be obtained in a multitude of shapes and weights, including some very small ones.

THERMOMETERS

Another must if you're that kind. Both the Taylor and the Hardy thermometers are good, but the Hardy is awfully fragile. Most biologists use the Taylor to check out water temperature. There have only been a couple of times when I was overwhelmed by not having one and a few other times when they made significant revelations.

Once I was led to a secret, just discovered, wonderful, etc., etc., etc., fishing stream in western Michigan. It was indeed lovely and slow-moving. My leader jumped out and began fishing. I diligently tried for an hour, got a bit paranoid and took the temperature. It was 78 degrees—long past any trout's nirvana.

STAFFS

Wading staffs can be useful or a real drag, depending on where you're wading and how. You can make one easily from an old ski pole that has some weight added at the bottom to point it through the current. The Orvis combination wading staff and rod case can be a fine convenience, but it's heavy as hell. There have

Turn-of-the-century reel case

been plenty of times when I needed a staff and had to improvise along the bank. If you have the money, go ahead and buy one. If you don't and if you face rough wading water, you should make one.

BOATS

The most popular fly-fishing boat is probably the rubber raft, but it isn't the best. It can be devilishly hard to maneuver in whitish water and dangerous for more than one person to fish from, but it is cheap, easy to set up and doesn't capsize often.

In running water, canoes are best, but it takes skill and practice to handle a canoe and a fly rod at the same time. The flat-bottomed boats used on Michigan's Au Sable and other Midwestern rivers are good to control and fish from, but aren't too good in white water.

The inner-tube contraptions that float one person around are okay for a cautious angler, but don't go too far out in a big, windy lake or you can get in over your head, literally.

CAMERAS

There are many fine little cameras like the Rollei, Leica CL and the top-of-the-line pocket Instamatics with glass rather than plastic lenses that fit easily and function well from your vest or bag. I prefer 35mm film because of its versatility. The ultra-miniatures like the Minox have been pretty much superseded by the new wave of little cameras. Their film size was just too small. Don't store your camera in a tight plastic bag for long periods of time because condensation can ruin it; but some sort of waterproof case is a necessity. Also, beware of keeping your camera in glove compartments—extreme heat can play havoc with film, especially color. If possible, use a fast film for fishing trips. Sometimes the real highlights of trips happen on toward dark, and you'll want film sensitive enough to record the happenings.

JOURNAL

If you don't keep a journal of your fishing trials and errors on a day-by-day basis, you are foolish. Religiously maintaining one will give your career as an angler continuity and history as nothing else can. It will become a wonderful source of practical information on hatches, tides and fish habits, telling you patterns of behavior that are unobtainable any other way, including the insights of angling gurus.

There are commercial ones available, but it is best to make your own from a small leather-bound loose-leaf notebook, season by season. At least, the commercial ones never seem to have exactly what I want to record, and their categories aren't mine.

GADGETRY

Just remember that many of the multitude of gadgets available serve little useful function and are much too expensive for mere frills.

19

What to Wear

Some years ago, on an unnamed but fancy Eastern river, Ed Zern, then an aspiring young angler, was flailing away after speckled beauties, wearing a pair of Levi's, a dark-colored T-shirt and sneakers.

That lordly aristocrat Edward Hewitt, heir to Grand Old Money in Grand Old Quantities and author of such noted classics as *A Trout and Salmon Fisherman for Seventy-Five Years*, approached gracefully along the bank decked out in his normal attire of tweeds. He watched Zern muck around in the water for a few moments then solemnly remarked, "Young man, one doesn't have to dress like a slob to catch trout."

Hewitt may have been right, but for many casual anglers the dictum that clothes make the man doesn't hold for their sport. Yet for some, a splendiferous minority in the post-Hewitt mode, clothes-consciousness is again becoming a fact of fishing. The fashions may be somewhat different from the tweed days, but they are fashions nonetheless.

Even as incorrigible a stream urchin as myself went through a minor peacock period, imitating the old order. It was back in Maryland where Peter Streett and I would wear secondhand tweed jackets when fishing, even for carp with doughballs. Perhaps it was more of a burlesque than an imitation. At any rate, this came to an abrupt halt on the frigid November day when Pete attempted to climb out of a rubber raft only to have it flip on him. When he emerged from his piscatorial baptism in waterlogged tweeds, he swore off the fancy duds and fished from then on in a rubber wet suit that he picked up from a retired scuba diver. "Extremism in the pursuit of fish is no vice," was his motto. It taught me a lesson and I kicked the fancy clothes, never forgetting that look of frozen anguish on Pete's face. Pragmatism and comfort are now my bywords, but I rarely get whistles on the stream any more.

For the ultra-tradition-minded angler, especially one fishing on gentle Eastern or Midwestern waters with little danger of drastic upsets, the formal regalia may be necessary for self-image. You pays your money and you takes your choice, as they say.

CLOTHING

Don't wear light or bright clothing. Unlike your personality, your clothing should be dull. Light has a way of reflecting off bright things, especially white, and I shudder when seeing trout or ocean flats fishermen in white T-shirts.

For fishing in places where you will get wet, the best material is cotton khaki. It dries rapidly. I'm normally a blue-jeans devotee, but they take forever to dry, especially when the sun goes down and you have to slog back to your car or camp. Some of the light cotton trousers let moisture evaporate so quickly you can almost see it.

Unless it's really hot, I don't like to wear short-sleeved shirts. Long ones help keep insects off and give you at least a minimal amount of protection from berserk casts. Also, at night in the mountains it cools very quickly, and a short-sleeved shirt that is comfortable in the daytime can get uncomfortable damn fast after dark.

I always take along a light Gerry back-packing raincoat in my bag, preferring a raincoat which has a zipper in front. The pullover types tend to steam you up when casting hard or hiking because they invariably have a poor ventilation system. Your light windbreaker coat should be as waterproof (not water resistant) as possible. You can tell the difference quickly in a downpour. Those 60/40 dual-material raincoats, like the Sierra designs, are hardly ever waterproof, though they can be comfortable to fish in on cool days.

In the spring and fall I take an Eddie Bauer down sweater with me. There have been many times when I was glad to have it. These sweaters weigh just a few ounces and will keep you warm

195

in anything short of a freak blizzard. If they get wet, however, they lose all their insulation properties, so you need the raincoat as well. Real wool sweaters can keep you warm even when wet, but they are heavier to haul around.

WADERS AND BOOTS

The most common thing one hears today is that there aren't any good waders. That may be true, but so much depends on how and where you fish that it's hard to generalize.

Dave Harriman, who has been raising fish and wearing waders in Montana for three decades, has one firm recommendation—get the commercial grade if you are going to splurge on good ones. Years of buying and repairing them have taught him that these models, not merchandised for sport fishermen but for hatchery people and other wading workers, last far longer and are usually cheaper. They can be bought through a number of stores specializing in such equipment.

Harriman also feels that the live-rubber waders are stronger than even the best canvas types you see advertised in catalogs, and he considers the old Ball Brand among the best ever. Most experienced steelheaders believe this, too. Some of the cheaper Japanese waders are made from live rubber, but they are often tight in the crotch, and that helps wear them out quickly. He says that experience indicates that the larger the size you can get away with, the longer they last. For example, he wears a size 11 shoe, but a size 13 wader backed up with extra socks lasts him much longer than a size 11 does.

There are generally two ways to go with waders. You can buy the better, more expensive American- or British-made ones and try to maintain them as long as possible, or you can get the cheap kind that are made in the sweatshops of Asia or Japan. If you go the less expensive route at $5 to $10 a pair, you will have to buy a couple of pairs a year if you aren't meticulous, and probably even if you are. But if a $40-to-$90 pair lasts you only a season or two, you aren't really ahead.

Something to remember is that nylon ages poorly. If the pair of waders you buy off the shelf has been resting there for a couple of years, they won't have a great life expectancy to begin with. Always find out their birth date if possible. Like doughnuts, waders should be fresh.

Sneakers resting after a day of wading

If you fish places where sharp rocks, barbed wire and other accident-causing items aren't commonplace, then you can get away with less expensive waders or, if money isn't your problem, whichever type is comfortable for you is best. I've found that the more elegant waders work and fit better, and if you wear 13's like me, you may find the same thing.

For most of my fishing years I've used stocking-foot waders rather than the boot-foots. I swapped for a pair of Russell wading brogues some seasons ago and wear them now. They are very comfortable, even with the stocking-foots inside them. Brogues could be worth their $50 price, but they can require an annual trip to the factory for a $10 overhaul. Stocking-foot waders are usually fragile, and I've yet to have a pair last me through even half a season. On the other hand, Ed Burlingame, the editor of this book, swears by Totes, a medium-priced stocking-foot that he wears with Converse wading sneakers. But Ed isn't the finicky type and probably could get by wearing Baggies on his feet. These waders, in the $15-to-$25 range, seem like a major compromise, and I would rather go to either price extreme than settle on them.

Something else I'm getting to appreciate more and more is hip boots. Except for people who are really good waders, most of us rarely go out above our crotch. In a fast river, deep wading can be an invitation to disaster. Also, chest waders can be an excuse for wading badly. When wearing hippers, you have to approach your target carefully and cast likewise. Some people with chest waders believe, erroneously, that they can blithely charge right up to suspected fish hangouts. (Speaking of disasters, please use a tight belt around the top of your chest waders in case of a spill. This way air stays in, which will keep you afloat, while water, which could drag you down the river, stays out.)

Hip boots are much cheaper than waders and can be carried around more easily. For most trout fishing the hippers can get you within range, and during hot weather they are much more comfortable than waders, which often get you wet from perspiration anyway.

The best thing for the bottom of waders, hip boots or wading shoes is felt and some sort of studs, preferably aluminum. But these drastic steps are required only for rough waters, moss bottoms or those killer slick rocks. Once on the Big Hole, with a 5-pound-plus brown on, I was stuck because I couldn't get any foot traction. Wearing only rubber-cleated Converse wading sneakers, every time I took a step to try to head the fish off, I fell. After a half hour of this a friend came to my rescue with his net. If he hadn't I might still be there, because I could never have let go. I'm about as graceful as a wading rhino and need the psychic comfort of felt and studs. For really treacherous water, such as steelheaders encounter, the bind-on metal chains or cleats are the final word in wading safety, but they are a bit much for general fishing.

The aforementioned Converse sneakers with felt bottoms, the Russells and, if you can ever find a pair, the luxurious Mills Wading Shoes are really good and fairly safe. If you can't find ones with felt on the bottom, kits are now available with felt cutouts. All-weather nylon carpet scraps work wonders as well when glued on and can be obtained free, or nearly free, from your friendly rug dealer. Barge cement is the best bonding agent.

For the past twenty years, I have waded bare during the summer, wherever I've fished. Wearing sneakers or brogues and shorts, I've jumped blithely into cool or tepid waters all around the country. Recently there have been some disquieting stories about the long-term effects of this activity on the circulation. Leonard Wright, in his *Fishing the Dry Fly as a Living Insect*, claims that this is the reason that Theodore Gordon suffered leg problems in his later life. But in talks with a number of physicians, I have not been able to get this corroborated. None of them has been able to figure out how and why damage would occur. It is possible you are taking a chance by wading bare, but there isn't any medical evidence to back the allegation up. All the doctors questioned, however, stressed that if you feel any symptoms of circulation problems you should stop wading bare immediately.

One other thing about waders and other such footgear. If you do rip them, don't use hot patches. They weaken the fabric around the rip because of the heat you have to apply. Use the regular cold bicycle patches. Rips can be detected by filling the wader or boot with air and placing under water. Look for telltale bubbles.

If your waders get wet inside, a portable hair drier works wonders, and a vacuum cleaner will do. If you have time and no electricity, fill the waders with newspaper and hang them upside down. (You should always hang them upside down anyway.) The paper will soak up the water slowly. After they have absorbed the bulk of the moisture, take the papers out and nature will do the rest.

HATS

For all-around use, the Orvis Year Rounder Helmet is good, but hats are a matter of taste far more than of practical consideration. The Year Rounder, which has gone up to $15, is made of a light but substantial cotton material and has a green underbrim to cut down on glare.

There are many similar hats for less money. Orvis's Norwegian Fisherman's Hat is very good also, especially for salt water. It has a big brim, tuck-away earflaps for stout breezes or driving rain, plastic pouches for whatevers and, most important, a mosquito-net accessory can be bought for it. I dyed my hat green, not liking the brightish brown color. Wool hats and caps, favored by some anglers, get a bit warm in midsummer. My own rule is, the brighter the sun the wider the brim should be.

INSECT REPELLENTS

I think Cutter's is best, but some disagree, preferring Off or other brands. The old-fashioned citronella worked fine, but it's as hard to get as pennyroyal, the traditional herbal remedy for biting insects. Dick and I sometimes smoke a God-awful mixture of Latakia and Perique tobaccos in mosquito country, which stinks terribly but keeps some of the biters away. Certain Italian cigars also do the trick, according to Robert Traver, but when you're really getting among those nasty critters, try to have mosquito netting. It works for sure. It is the only item that will really keep them off.

The main problem with the sprays and lotions is that the repellents which keep the bugs away don't seem to stay on your skin, and the stuff that stays on your skin seems to be bug hors d'oeuvres. If you are sweating it right off, it may help to mix a little vaseline with your Cutter's or any other expensive antibug stuff.

SUNGLASSES

You really need some sort of light-polarizing glasses, such as Polaroid. Others will cut down the glare a little, but the Polaroid types are head and shoulders above anything else. They also allow you to peek into the water better than the others. Be careful cleaning the plastic ones, as you can scratch them almost by staring at them. Always wet the tissue or whatever else you're using to clean them before applying it to the surface. I don't think that the very fancy fish-seeing type of sunglasses offers much more than Polaroids.

20
The Written Tradition

I

A very important part of any angler's equipment should be the literature of the sport, both historic and modern. To neglect the classics is to neglect much of the joy of fishing.

Angling is a combination of theory and practice, each making possible the advancement of the other. From the theoretical musings come ideas for the actual fishing experience, and out of the experience comes more theory. So it has been since the first fly was thrown at a fish dumb enough to take it. Ignorance of the traditions and history of angling would rob us of the pleasure of knowing how we got from where we were to where we are. It would also limit our insight about where we are going.

There is a certain amount of knowledge of the sport that can be described as basic, which can be garnered from the literature. Like any other "tackle," the choice of books is ultimately arbitrary and subjective, but a few helpful guidelines can help make some sense from the morass. Unlike the rest of our gear, our choices of books are best viewed from a historical perspective, rather than as isolated volumes with different degrees of practicality.

But there are difficulties in looking over our literature. The basic problem with American fly-fishing literature is found in the practice of American fly-fishing—much of it takes place in the shadow of the bulldozer. Environmental destruction has been a haunting specter to this country's angler since the beginning of this century.

Our English trout-fishing cousins are secure in the knowledge that their fishing rivers have remained basically the same for hundreds of years. What Walton wrote about fishing the Dove in *The Compleat Angler* in 1754 still has a great deal of relevance to a British angler in 1975. But what an American writer hurriedly says about his favorite river today may be completely obsolete next week because of environmental destruction. The English pattern of land ownership, under which control of the famed chalk streams is rigidly maintained by wealthy people, is very different from that in our country, where the freestone streams with their assorted headwaters have mostly eluded the grasp of our wealthier anglers. It is comparatively easy to own completely a meadowland spring creek with an identifiable beginning and end. It is another matter to own an American stream with scores of potentially pollution-bearing tributaries.

This sense of destruction and its accompanying anxiety have perverted much of American fishing literature. If today's beloved river is going to be tomorrow's shopping center or pesticide dump, what is a poor author to do? The general response to this major dilemma has taken two forms. The most prevalent one, which appears in most of the thousands of American fly-fishing books, is to search out a previously untapped gimmick or gadget to exploit fishing in a new location. This can be geographic or by the development of tackle that would reach specific areas in a lake or river. This includes such gambits as fishing in Alaska or British Columbia; fishing deeper; fishing a new kind of fly; casting farther; etc. The writer engages in a race against time to gather his fish while he may. Some fine books have been written in this manner, but they become dated very quickly, depending as they do on technical advances in tackle rather than the historical accumulation of knowledge.

The other category has a definite long-range value. These are the books trafficking in a kind of melancholia. Their general mood was summed up for me in a Federation of Fly Fishing Clubs conclave speech in which Lee Wulff exclaimed, "The fishing will never again be as good as it is this moment." This attitude mirrors a passiveness in the face of change for the worse, a sullen acceptance of things as they are becoming. It has characterized many recent writers who see little to be optimistic about or look forward to. The good days are gone forever and there is nothing to be done.

The most extreme example of this angling despair appears in the nontechnical material that Ernie Schwiebert, author of the classic *Matching the Hatch,* has produced over the past decade. It always seems to be twilight in his angling world, and he has written as if he were eighty ever since he was twenty. This school of angling writers—the other side of the try-new-things coin—often writes in self-pitying ways, impotent in the face of our current environmental mishmash. One group exploits our love of gimmicks and the other group exploits our despair.

But these people, like those in many trout conservation organizations, are faced with a paradox. The luxuries and privileges of the wealthy have been purchased, in large measure, with our trout streams, bass rivers and ocean estuaries. We have paid too steep a price for our cars, shopping centers and television—for the mentality that insists we need more of everything. Time is running out for all these things—and us as well—if we don't start choosing more wisely. We can't support both our fishing habits and our luxury habit, spawned by an economic system predicated on waste and greed. It is past the time to kid ourselves, and that is the problem with these maudlin writers. They act as if it is a mystery why the fishing ain't as good as it was. We know and they know. It's time to put up or shut up.

II

A basic fishing library should consist of books in three general categories, though the best overlap all groups.

Under the first heading are the more or less technical books, telling us about the basic skills required to fool fish, most especially trout. We have to eliminate the gimmick books, which either try to bluff us or to blow a minor angling scheme up into a way of life. Most fishing books just repeat or refine what the basic books say. There have been thousands of angling books in the past five hundred years, and few have done more than add a fact or two to the body of knowledge that comprises the sport. Once we get past those without much substance, we uncover a small group that tells most of what we should know about trout fishing, as it is practiced today.

The next group is the historic books which are significant because they were the major building blocks in getting fly-fishing where it is at. Sometimes it's difficult to tell which current books are really important because of their immediacy, but, as we look back over history, certain volumes stand out vividly in contrast to the run-of-the-mill publications. Who can know what books written during our current fly-fishing revival will be considered important from the perspective of one hundred years hence? Perhaps it will be a book obscure today, and the best-sellers will be remembered only by angling scholars. A prophet is never glorified in his own time, as they say.

The third group is made up of the more spiritual books. They provide the sport's "theology." This is a traditional part of fly-fishing literature, in a continuous line from the first book, *The Treatyse of Fysshynge Wyth an Angle,* written in the mid-fifteenth century. Dame Juliana Berners reserved sections of that treatyse to speak of the ethical glories of fishing and its superiority over other field sports. We, in our more fragmented way, sometimes reserve whole books for our memoirs, reminiscences, lies and thoughts on angling. When these books are bad, they are awful. The excesses occurred in the late nineteenth century, when proper English gentlemen, in late Romantic style, felt impelled to inform us of their lives afield. Recently there have been similar attempts in this country to vie for the honors in turgidity. These books can be pure poetry, however, under the right conditions, and the best examples are as sweetly written as almost anything else in our language. (I hope Shakespeare and Melville will forgive me.)

I have read a few hundred fishing books and have scanned perhaps a thousand. The lists that follow seem to be the cream of them all, but they are only a starting place for anyone deeply interested in the literature of the sport. Since most flycasters, throughout history, have been from the ranks of the haves rather than the have-nots, many fine books were issued in limited editions or privately printed, and some are very difficult to find. I've tried to include only books at least semireadily available, though it forces omissions of some outstanding works.

TECHNICAL WORKS

Trout, Ray Bergman. This book has been in print almost continuously since its original publication in 1937. It is as close to a still-read American classic as we have, and it has managed to avoid the usual pitfalls. It was written after the introduced brown trout generally supplanted our native brookie—a victim of watershed manipulation around the turn of the century. *Trout* was also written before the kamikaze assault on our resources that has occurred since the war, so, being betwixt and between, it has a timelessness missing from most of our literature. It deals with all the major issues facing trout fishermen and is probably the best primer on the sport. Another plus factor is that it is written in a very mellow style.

Trout Fishing, Joe Brooks. *Trout Fishing* is the last book Brooks wrote, and it's a fine compendium of modern fly-fishing techniques, especially for the beginner in the West who is not hung up on exact-imitation dry flies. Brooks was a devotee of the power-fishing school of angling, but covers almost everything one needs to know to get along under all sorts of circumstances.

The Trout and the Stream, Charles Brooks. Charlie Brooks has been trying to systematize big-fish fishing in Western rivers for quite a while. His crude tackle, consisting of rough rods, sinking lines and somewhat grotesque flies, will shock the sensibilities of refined Easterners and other classicists, but they work. Brooks is an ingenious tactician and has a feel for his angling studies. His work has become more and more important as Brooks's home in the West Yellowstone region has become the last major holdout for big river trout in the country. His ideas could be thought of as a major extension of Joe Brooks's theories.

Fishing the Dry Fly as a Living Insect, Leonard Wright. Wright's basic thesis is that the more hardy caddis fly has become the dominant trout insect food, replacing our old friend the mayfly, which is an early victim of water-quality deterioration. His ideas—written as well as one could want—lead him to musings on tackle, fly handling and just about everything else an Eastern angler could want. It's a very important book, but not as widely circulated as some lesser efforts. It might be a little advanced for the basic trainee, however.

Streamside Guide, Art Flick. This book has been reprinted and sold many copies. It was the first work to try to systematize insect hatches. Though Flick worked on upstate New York insects, basically mayflies, his methodology remains important to hatch matching in general. Beginners can learn the imitationist ropes from this short work.

A Modern Dry Fly Code, Vincent Marinaro. Marinaro's book was the first American work to deal with spring-creek fishing as a separate activity. Many books on limestone fishing have recently come out, but it remains the most important. Some of his ideas in this early-50's publication, first issued as a limited edition, are dated, but its essence remains as valid as ever. This book is the foundation of modern spring-creek fishing.

Some other books that are important, though not cornerstones of modern technique, are:

Matching the Hatch, Ernie Schwiebert. A blending and extension of Preston Jennings's *A Book of Flies* and Art Flick's *Streamside Guide.* Schwiebert's *Nymphs* is also an important work, but the fly patterns are too technical and overcomplicated, and he offers no adequate instructions for tying them. The illustrations of naturals are very nice.

Selective Trout, Carl Richards and Doug Swisher. They try to deal with mayflies, mostly on spring creeks, in this book. It is an important work which develops the idea of hackleless dries to new heights. Its applicability is somewhat limited, however.

How to Fish from Top to Bottom, Sid Gordon. This book is worth reading if you can locate a copy. It is about the only book that attempts to deal with fishing from a biologist's perspective.

HISTORICAL WORKS

The Complete Fly Fisherman: The Notes and Letters of Theodore Gordon, John McDonald. Gordon was the founder of our dry-fly fishing, and he's as important a figure in this country's angling as there is. He is a delight to read about from any perspective, and his only fault was that he wrote nothing except letters and columns for magazines. McDonald is a superb historian of angling and helps breathe life into his subject.

History of Fly Fishing for Trout, John Waller Hills. This is *the* book on the history of the sport. It's well written and has everything that anyone except a scholar needs to know about angling from its beginnings in England until the turn of the twentieth century. You should not miss it.

The Dry Fly and Fast Water, George LaBranche. This 1914 book marked the true beginnings of the unique American fly-fishing tradition. LaBranche weaned us away from English traditions, and the style he uses to discuss our angling conditions and needs is second to none.

Dry Fly Fishing, Frederick Halford. This was the true beginning of the floating fly, which had appeared and disappeared throughout history before this work came out in the late 1880's. Halford was stuffy and somewhat dogmatic, but he certainly knew in what direction we were heading.

The Way of a Trout with a Fly, G. E. M. Skues. This is the book in which the nymph emerged in its modern form. Branded heresy when it appeared in the 1920's by some of the more zealous dry-fly followers of Halford, it pointed the way for modern nymph fishing.

A Trout and Salmon Fisherman for Seventy-Five Years, Edward Hewitt. Hewitt was the major figure in American angling from the deaths of Gordon and LaBranche to the postwar and modern days. He was an aristocratic Eastern gentleman, usually fishing private waters, but he knew every aspect of the sport and played an important role in determining the directions we took after his long life.

"LITERARY" WORKS

The Compleat Angler, Izaak Walton. Walton's immortal book is actually more of a flowery literary work than any sort of angler's guide. Its language can be a bit much, but all the current ethical arguments about fishing go directly back to it. Probably the best-known and least-read book around. The fly-fishing section in the fifth edition, written by Walton's friend Charles Cotton, is outstanding.

Trout Madness, Robert Traver. A fine book from the 1960's that differentiated itself from the others by its light style in the memoir idiom, in place of the usual seriousness about our sport. Its humorous anecdotes are classic fish stories by a lifelong flycaster who was neither an "outdoor writer" nor an "expert."

A River Never Sleeps, Roderick Haig-Brown. This book blends the best of the British tradition with the best of the American. Haig-Brown, who writes from Vancouver Island, was the first West Coaster to develop a national angling writing reputation and is with little doubt the best writer on the sport this continent has yet produced. His chronicle of the natural history of a river has yet to be matched.

Fishing Widows, Nick Lyons. The best of the modern sensibility books. Lyons writes about angling in a broad social context from his position as a trapped New Yorker with all of the urbanite's usual dreams and frustrations. He is a polished stylist who knows how to express what so many of us feel. Humor and understanding help overcome the sadness that surfaces from time to time.

Most of the fine nineteenth-century works by people like William Scropes are out of print, but they are a pleasure if you can get hold of them. John Taintor Foote, who is also out of print, is very fine in things like *The Wedding Gift* and *Fishermen All*.

For salmon anglers, Lee Wulff's *Atlantic Salmon* still stands out from the other North American books.

Steelheaders have been getting more books to paw through recently. Among the available ones, *Steelhead Trout* by Trey Combs and *Steelhead* by Mel Marshall top the list.

The recent *Fly Fishing in Salt Water* by Lefty Kreh is the most satisfactory description of a sport that has yet to be organized as rigorously as trout fishing.

For the other aspects of the sport—i.e., bass, panfish and the like—you will have to look around carefully. Nothing really stands out as basic equipment for the angler.

Afterword:

That's All, Folks

Winter is about over in Western Montana. You can feel the season change slowly with the winds, and the snow is beginning to melt its way back up the mountains.

It is the time of year to begin stirring, to check over tackle and catalogs and the lists of new books. It is also the time of year to wonder what this season will bring and nervously wonder what damage has been done to our favorite waters since we saw them last.

This is the same world where starvation and despair is the undeserved lot of many people, but where there yet remains some space for clear rivers and solitude. Crisis defines our way of life, but there is still a little time to ponder gently which mayfly a trout favors. It is a season to become aware of these contradictions and to understand what they mean.

We can never preserve the sweet waters and fertile ocean flats while our neglected cities decay. We will never save the multitudes of fish while there are people still going hungry. One infects the other like a virulent disease. Our urban areas are as much a part of our total ecosystem as the trout stream we are fighting to save. If we blindly ignore one of them, then there can be no real hope of saving the other. We are all wrapped up in this together and must sink or swim that way.

This is the true message of angling. It is no accident that angling has inspired religious feelings since its beginnings. Its underlying theology or message is that everything is connected ultimately. The trout and the stone-fly nymph form one connection—

and so does the pesticide factory upstream with its stockholders clamoring for dividends. Every living thing touches every other, and the circle must remain unbroken if we are to survive. If you disturb one part of this delicate structure, then someone or something must pay the price somewhere along the line. It is this high price we are paying today for our pride and greed.

By fishing, we are participating in the entire process of life on earth, not escaping it. We are just seeing one of the best parts. If we have to separate our lives into estranged categories of fisherman, student, businessman, or whatever else, a great price has to be paid physically for this fragmentation of our being. When we carefully stalk a fish we are human beings in direct communion with the natural world—a part of the whole world. To ignore your role in this whole process is to ignore the most satisfying part of it.

Tackle is a part of this process. Many of my strongest friendships have been constructed around a common interest in the tools of angling. Richard Eggert in Kalamazoo and a small rod; Robert Traver in Ishpeming, Michigan, and a dozen No. 28 flies; Richard Brautigan and a Winston rod in Pine Creek, Montana; Tom Mc-Guane and a Paul Young Perfectionist in Livingston; Russ Chatham and a Perfect reel at Pine Creek; Nick Lyons and books in New York; Marshall Bloom and Wynn Rainbolt and a lovely Payne in Hamilton.

Though these items were the catalysts for the initial encounters, like the clothes a woman wears or the way a man parts his hair, they were quickly superseded, and the friendships were cemented together by human values, not by the attraction of some commodity—which, after all, is what all equipment, even the finest, is. The most important things to share are the common experiences and feelings that make us people and of which fishing and its artifacts are important parts for many of us. The basic difference between the $10 discount-house rod and the superb Garrison can't be measured in any intrinsic terms. The difference is the human care, experience and tradition which went into their making.

Tackle is an expression of these things which I prize so deeply. Only that and nothing more.

Appendix A:

Instant Gratification

Despite everything that's been said and done, you just have to have a bit of instant tackle gratification. You've just received a call from a long-lost buddy who made a fortune investing in used bamboo rods in the early 1960's and he's invited you along for "the fishing trip of a lifetime." His private jet is going to be landing on your roof in an hour and you have to run out and buy some exotic tackle. (If we're going to fantasize, let's go all the way.)

The following are simply my own personal choices for basic outfits for most types of fishing available. They show nakedly all the prejudices I've been trying to hide throughout this book. They are, once again, the choices I—and no one else—would make in each bracket. I'm not going to go to the wall over them either, so save your breath!

The first outfit under each heading is one that is about as cheap as can be found in the category these days, still in the neighborhood of $50 or so with the Cortland 444 and Scientific Angler sinker that fits. The second outfit listed is for the moderate-priced outfit, these days around $100 bare. The third item is the supertackle, and I won't even hazard a guess as to cost. For the less expensive spreads, I would use Berkeley Leaders, and Orvis or Leonard for the others. No skimping on the line or the flies needed for the undertakings, and at least one book, as listed, should go along, too.

BASIC OUTFIT

Fenwick 8-foot, No. 6 line, Heddon-imported Japanese imitation of Hardy Lightweight reel

Winston 8-foot, No. 6 line, Pflueger Medalist reel
Paul Young Para 15, 8-foot, No. 6 line, Hardy Princess reel
McClane's New Standard Fishing Encyclopedia, Al McClane

LIGHT TROUT

Leonard Rangely 7-foot, No. 5 line, Heddon-imported Japanese
    imitation of Hardy Lightweight reel
Scientific Angler System 4, 7-foot-2-inch, No. 4 line, Orvis Madison
    reel
Leonard Au Sable 39, 7½-foot, Walker t/R 3 reel
Trout Fishing, Joe Brooks

HEAVY TROUT

Cortland 8½-foot, No. 8 line, Pflueger reel
Vince Cummins River Rat 8-foot, No. 8 line, Berkeley Custom 2 reel
Winston Bamboo 8½-foot, No. 7 line, Hardy Zenith Multiplier reel
The Trout and the Stream, Charles Brooks

SALMON

Berkeley 8-foot, No. 7 line, Pflueger reel
Orvis Golden Eagle 9-foot, No. 9 line, Scientific Angler System
    9 reel
Leonard Miramachi 8½-foot, No. 8 line, Bogdan reel
Atlantic Salmon, Lee Wulff

STEELHEAD

Phillipson 8½-foot, No. 9 line, Pflueger reel
Winston 9-foot, No. 9 line, Hardy Husky Multiplier reel
Peak 9-foot, No. 9 line, Bogdan reel
Steelhead Trout, Trey Combs

SALT WATER

Phillipson 8½-foot, No. 9 line, Pflueger reel
Scientific Angler System 10, Orvis Salt Water reel
Peak 9½-foot, No. 10 line, Bogdan reel
Fly Fishing in Salt Water, Lefty Kreh

PANFISH AND SMALL BASS

Cortland 2000, 7½-foot, No. 6 line, Pflueger reel
Fenwick 7-foot, No. 6 line, Orvis Madison reel
Orvis Wes Jordan 7½-foot, No. 6 line, Hardy Princess Multiplier
    reel
Nothing special written.

BACKPACKING

Eagle Claw 8-foot, No. 7 line, Pflueger Medalist reel
Winston four-piece 8-foot, No. 6 line, Hardy Princess reel
Peak four-piece 8-foot, No. 6 line, Hardy Princess reel
Nothing special written for backpack fishing.

As a last thought, anyone who buys tackle from a list such as this should be flogged mercilessly with a medium-action, steelhead rod and spend a few dollars talking to a psychiatrist about being compulsive.

Appendix B:

Tools of the Trade—How to Buy Tackle

The following lists contain many of the more important locations for buying tackle, though surely not all. This is a changing market; some of the addresses will soon be out of date, and some of the omissions will become glaring.

I have tried to emphasize what each outfit sells that is unique —or at least special—and whatever else I can succinctly add. Most fly shops these days carry a complete line of equipment.

REELS

Aladdin Mfg. Co.
620 S. 8th Street
Minneapolis, Minn. 55404

Mostly automatic reels, but some rods, too

Daiwa Corporation
14011 S. Normandie Avenue
Gardena, Calif. 90247

Some okay Japanese imports, including less-okay rods

Feuer Brothers, Inc.
77 Lafayette Avenue
White Plains, N.Y. 10603

Some very fine large fly reels suited for salt water, steelhead and the like

Martin Reel Company, Inc.
30 E. Main Street
Mohawk, N.Y. 13407

One of the oldest names in automatics, plus rods and fly boxes

Northwest Cast Metal Products
2138 N.W. 29th
Portland, Oreg. 97210

Manufacturers of the Colgrove reel

Pflueger Corporation
P.O. Box 310
Hallandale, Fla. 33009

The standard American "lineholders" for decades now, plus other things not as interesting.

Rogue Reels, Inc.
2912 South River Road
Grants Pass, Oreg. 97526

A favorite reel of some of the cultish steelheaders

Seamaster Fishing Reels
4615 Le Jeune Road
Coral Gables, Fla. 33146

Superb big-game fly reels, alleged to be the best ever made

Tycoon Fin-Nor
29 Essex Street
Maywood, N. J. 07607

Another of the very expensive stainless-steel, mainly big-game reels; a contender for the best-constructed reel on the market

Val-Craft, Inc.
671 North Worcester Street
Chartley, Mass. 02712

They make the interesting-looking Valentine fly reel

Arthur L. Walker & Son, Inc.
P.O. Box 249
Hempstead, N.Y. 11550

A very nice line of reels from small trout to multiplying salmon

RODS

Angler's Mail
6497 Pearl Road
Cleveland, Ohio 44130

They import boodles of English bamboo rods, plus lots of other nice accessories

Berkeley & Co.
Highways 9 and 71
Spirit Lake, Iowa 51360

Getting snazzy with their rods since hackleless Doug Swisher came aboard, as they say

Browning Arms Co.
Route 1
Morgan, Utah 84050

These high-powered people are now into rods, plus other fly things

Farlow & Co., Ltd.
213 Regal Exchange
London, EC 3, England

Bamboo rods of various value to Yanks

Garcia Corp.
329 Alfred Avenue
Teaneck, N.J. 07666

Big producer of lots of mass rods, plus some fairly interesting reels

Horrocks-Ibbotson
20 Whitesboro
Utica, N.Y. 13502

Inexpensive rods, etc., from this longtime outfit

H. L. Leonard Rod Co.
25 Cottage Street
Midland Park, N.J. 07432

Alas, Leonard just recently moved its headquarters from its venerable New York address after over a hundred years, although Leonard rods are still being made in Central Valley, N.Y.

Russ Peak
21 North Allen Avenue
Pasadena, Calif. 91106

The finest glass rods ever custom-made—the best-finished rods in the country today, bar none—anything your little casting arm could want

Pezon & Michel
21 Route De Tours
37400 Amboise, France

Full parabolic bamboo and some glass, designed by meticulous Charles Ritz

Powell Rod Co.
1148 W. 8th Avenue
Chico, Calif. 95926

Son Walton carries on E. C.'s tradition, but without the emphasis on the bamboo. Fine fiberglass rods, almost bargains at their prices

St. Croix Corp.
9909 S. Shore Drive
Minneapolis, Minn. 55441

An inexpensive line of rods

Sevenstrand Tackle Mfg. Co.
748 Lincoln
Westminster, Calif. 92683

They make the giant-selling Fenwick rods, have a complete line including graphites

Shakespeare Co.
241 E. Kalamazoo Avenue
Kalamazoo, Mich. 49006

Best bet is their fine graphite—but they have a full line of things

South Bend Tackle Co.
South Otselic, N.Y. 13155

An old-timer having trouble with making solid new-time rods plus other things

Thomas and Thomas
4 Fiske Avenue
Greenfield, Mass. 01301

Vast array of bamboo rods from this newcomer to the rod business

True Temper Corp.
1623 Euclid Avenue
Cleveland, Ohio 44115

Better their axes than their inexpensive fly rods

Uslan Rod Mfg. & Sales Co.
18679 W. Dixie Highway
North Miami Beach, Fla. 33160

The old Uslan five-sided bamboo rods have been recently reborn with a Florida address

R. L. Winston Rod Co.
475 Third Street
San Francisco, Calif. 94107

The favored old California bamboo builder changed hands and is emphasizing fine glass now

Wright & McGill Co.
4245 E. 46th Avenue
Denver, Colo. 80216

Line of inexpensive rods with big-selling backpacker

Paul H. Young
14039 Peninsula Drive
Traverse City, Mich. 49684

Master builder Bob Sommers and Jack Young carry on admirably in Paul's tradition of making great casting rods

LINES

Cortland Line Co.
Cortland, N.Y. 13045

About the best fly lines made, plus rods, reels, boxes and whatevers

Gladding
5101 N.W. 36th Avenue
Miami, Fla. 33166

Pretty fair fly lines, plus some other things

Mason Tackle Co.
Otisville, Mich. 48463

Old leader and nylon material company

Newton Line Co.
150 S. Main Street
Homer, N.Y. 13077

Nice fly lines

Scientific Anglers, Inc.
Box 2001
Midland, Mich. 48640

Brought synthetic lines out of the Dark Ages, still outstanding; good basic rods, reels

Sunset Line & Twine Co.
Petaluma, Calif. 94952

Masterweave fly lines loved by some

SECONDHAND TACKLE

Martin J. Keane
Mine Hill Road
Bridgewater, Conn. 06752

The granddaddy of the used-rod salesmen—good-sized lists

Roger Lampman
817 Orman Drive
Boulder, Calif. 80303

Buys, sells and deals the nice C. W. Jenkins cane rods designed on Garrison tapers

Bob Lee
16 E. 53rd Street
New York, N.Y. 10022

Anton Udwary, Jr.
1432-B Dover Road
Spartanburg, S.C. 29301

Buys, sells, trades and handles some new things

GENERAL FISHING TACKLE

Abercrombie & Fitch
Madison Avenue and 45th Street
New York, N.Y. 10017

Joining the Plastic Generation, but still plenty of nice fly tackle

Eddie Bauer
1737 Airport Way South
Seattle, Wash. 98134

Beautiful catalog of down-filled sportswear, plus lots of intermediate-priced tackle

L. L. Bean, Inc.
Freeport, Maine 04032

One of the original suppliers for outdoorsmen, changed little in this epoch; fine catalog

Cabela's, Inc.
812 13th Avenue
Sidney, Nebr. 69162

Lots of low-priced fly tackle and some bargains

Len Codella's Angler's Den
5 South Wood Avenue
P.O. Box 701
Linden, N.J. 07036

Buys, sells used rods, plus offering one of the best catalogs of fly-fishing accessories anyone is putting out; multitude of rods, reels, etc.; high-quality stuff

The Fly Fisherman's Bookcase Tackle Service
Route 9-A
Croton-on-Hudson, N.Y. 10520

Excellent line of just about everything in a first-class catalog at bargain prices

Hardy Brothers, Ltd.
61 Pall Mall
London, SW 1, England

Lots of things, but sure not like the good old days

Herter's
R.R. 2
Mitchell, S.D. 57301

The Ringling Brothers of inexpensive tackle; incredible catalog

McHardy's
9 London Road
Carlisle, England

Big catalog for $1 that offers potpourri of stuff

Netcraft Company
3101 Sylvania Avenue
Toledo, Ohio 43613

General store for myriad of tackle trinkets; okay catalog

The Orvis Company
Manchester, Vt. 05254

Juicy catalog featuring their bamboo rods, but including everything else under the sun

Norm Thompson
1805 N.W. Thurman Street
Portland, Oreg. 97209

Fancy things for the would-be elegant

FLIES AND TIERS

Adelphi Mill Flies
P.O. Box 788 (Dept. SA)
Adelphi Mills, Md. 20783

Dan Bailey Fly Shop
209 West Park Street
Livingston, Mont. 59047

Pioneer Western fly shop, fine flies, excellent catalog of everything swell

Randy Berry's Flies
Box 401
Teton Valley Lodge
Driggs, Idaho 83422

W. Coffey
384 St. James Street West
Montreal, Quebec

Harry Darbee
Livingston Manor, N.Y. 12758

Classic American tier out of Rube Cross tradition

Esmond Drury, Ltd.
Langton by Spilsby
Lincolnshire, England

Glen L. Evans, Inc.
Caldwell, Idaho 83605

Black's Custom Flies
Box 95
North Umpqua Highway
Roseburg, Oreg. 97470

Poul Jorgensen
604 Providence Road
Towson, Md. 21204

Author-tier of some exquisite creations for salt water and fresh

Jorgensen Brothers
4225 Stanley Boulevard
Pleasanton, Calif. 94566

Kaufman's Streamborn Flies
P.O. Box 23032
Portland, Oreg. 97233

Keel Fly
Box 8499
Toledo, Ohio 43623

The upside-down, at least semisnagless flies

Bud Lilly's Trout Shop
West Yellowstone, Mont. 59758

Fine, expensive Whitlock Western flies and good catalog of mountain trout gear

Patrick's Fly Shop
2237 Eastlake Avenue
Seattle, Wash. 98104

Steelhead flies, plus fine basic books on tying and other stuff

Poulsen Quality Flies
73 N.E. 43rd Avenue
Portland, Oreg. 97213

Steelhead flies and tackle

Hank Roberts
Box 308
1033 Walnut Street
Boulder, Colo. 80302

Rogan of Donegal
Ballyshannon Co.
Donegal, Ireland

Nice salmon flies plus rods, etc., for the American trade

Colin and Alex Simpson
34 Seamount Court
Gallowgate, Aberdeen
Scotland

Steelheaders Supply House
17284 S.E. Oatfield Road
Milwaukie, Oreg. 97222

Percy Tackle
28 Monument Square
Portland, Maine 04111

E. Veniard
138 Northwood Road
Thornton Heath
Surrey, England

Flies and tying stuff; nice catalog

Weber Tackle Company
1039 Ellis Street
Stevens Point, Wis. 54481

Old-timer still hanging in there

Jimmy Younger
Southerland Fly, Ltd.
Helmsdale, Scotland

NETS

Ed Cummins, Inc.
2305 Branch Road
Flint, Mich. 48506

ROD REPAIR

Try the original manufacturer if possible. If not, write to any of the bamboo builders such as Paul Young, Winston, Leonard, Orvis, Thomas and so on. Write and describe malady before sending.

ROD BLANKS

Angling Specialities
Box 97
Ancaster, Ont. 19g-313

Dale Clemens Custom Tackle
Route 3, Box 415-F
Allentown, Pa. 18104

Clemens wrote a book on glass-rod construction and knows his stuff

Depew Mfg. Corp.
359 Duffy Avenue
Hicksville, N.Y. 11801

Finny Sports
4910 Glanzman Road
Toledo, Ohio 43614

Nice catalog with blanks and materials and low-priced tackle

E. Hille
Williamsport, Pa. 17701

COMMERCIAL-GRADE WADERS

McNary's Farm Supply
Lonoke, Ark. 72086

Also:

Sears Roebuck and Co.

FLY-TYING GEAR

Creative Sports Enterprises
5831 Pacheco Boulevard
Pacheco, Calif. 94553

Necks and materials

Gudebrod Brothers Silk Co., Inc.
12 S. 12th Street
Philadelphia, Pa. 19107

Complete wrapping and winding supplies

O. Mustad & Son (USA), Inc.
185 Clark Street
Auburn, N.Y. 13021

The biggest quality hooker in the country—imported from Norway

Streamside Anglers
Box 2158
Missoula, Mont. 59801

Very knowledgeable with fur and feathers, fine necks; informative catalog

FLY BOXES

Fye Fly Boxes
Richardson's
Osceola Mills, Pa. 16666

A full line, plus custom-made metal-shelved boxes worn around the neck in lieu of a vest

FLY-FISHING SHOPS

This is just a sprinkling of the specialty and semispecialty shops around the country that have varying qualities of equipment but are all good sources of information on the available angling— and whatever else you need to know.

Anglers Nook
Box 57a
Shushan, N.Y. 12873

Anglers Pro Shop
Box 35
Springfield, Ohio 45501

The Barbless Hook
23 N.W. 23rd Place
Portland, Oreg. 97210

Betts Tackle, Ltd.
P.O. Box 57
Highway 42 West
Fuquay Varina, N.C. 27526

Black Hills Fly Shop
Box 616
Hill City, S.D. 57745

Hackle House
Fremont, California 94536

Jim's Fishing Gallery
24033 6 Place West
Bothell, Wash. 98011

The Millpond
59 North Santa Cruz Avenue
Los Gatos, Calif. 95030

Some fine anglers are
associated with this new store

Rangeley Region Sports Shop
Box 850
Rangeley, Maine 04970

The Rod and Reel
P.O. Box 132
Leola, Pa. 17540

Bodmer's Fly Shop
2400 Neagele Road
Colorado Springs, Colo. 80904

Don's Tackle Shop
7622 S.E. Foster Road
Portland, Oreg. 97206

Fireside Anglers, Inc.
P.O. Box 823
Melville, N.Y. 11746

The Fly Fisherman's
   Bookcase Tackle Service
Route 9-A
Croton-on-Hudson, N.Y. 10520

Hackle and Tackle
553 N. Salina
Syracuse, N.Y. 13208

Sunken Fly
Box 2
Provincetown, Mass. 02657

Sunrise Sports Center
P.O. Box 2003
Rochester, N.H. 03867

World Wide Sportsman, Inc.
P.O. Box 46
Islamorada, Fla. 33036

Yellow Breeches Fly Shop
Box 205
Boiling Springs, Pa. 17007

Ed Koch, spring-creek
specialist, is in charge here

BOOKS

Anglers & Shooters Bookshelf
Goshen, Conn. 06756

Big-time used-book dealer with very large catalog of listings

British Book Center, Inc.
153 East 78th Street
New York, N.Y. 10021

The Fly Fisherman's Bookcase
Route 9-A
Croton-on-Hudson, N.Y. 10520

Lots of the current book offerings plus large catalog of every type of fly-fishing gear

Sporting Book Service
Box 181
Rancocas, N.J. 08073

Harmon Henkin fishing in Post Creek
in his front yard in the Mission Valley

Appendix C:

Fly-Fishing Tackle Books

Almost every book written on fishing over the last five hundred years has dealt with tackle to a greater or lesser—usually lesser—degree, but there have been few books which have ever dealt with that subject specifically. The following list, given in chronological order, contains books that have a good deal to say on the subject or have said something that is unique. Many of them are out of print and rather difficult and expensive to obtain, but that is always a problem for those interested in the past.

These books as a whole will give a sense of the development of tackle from its early stages down to today.

Berners, Dame Juliana, *Treatyse of Fysshynge Wyth an Angle.* Circa 1494.

This earliest fishing work lists complete directions for making the tackle of the day.

Denny, John, *Secrets of Angling.* 1613.

Another early work with details of the home tackle building of the day.

Ronalds, Alfred, *The Fly Fisher's Entomology.* London: Longman, Rees, 1836.

Important work on the development of flies and the first to deal with representative patterns.

Henshall, James, *The Book of the Black Bass.* Cincinnati: Robert Clarke & Company, 1881.

Very important study of the bamboo rod in the United States, plus other nice stuff.

Wells, Henry P., *Fly Rods and Fly Tackle*. New York: Harper & Brothers, 1885.
The first theoretical book on American tackle, with details on the early days of the split-cane rod.

Keene, John Harrington, *Fishing Tackle*. London: Ward & Locke, 1886.
An English version of Wells, but not as interesting, since the rod hadn't reached the same high level over there.

Halford, Frederick, *Dry Fly Fishing*. London: Barry Shurlock reprint, 1973 (original published 1889).
Good treatment of early dry-fly tackle, especially rods.

Camp, Samuel G., *Fishing Kits and Equipment*. London: Outing Publishing Company, 1910.
Rather pedestrian but interesting general coverage.

Holden, George Parker, *Idyll of the Split Bamboo*. Stuart & Kidd, 1920.
Discussion of the theory of bamboo rod building; Holden developed the five-sided construction idea.

Hills, John Waller, *A History of Fly Fishing for Trout*. Rockville Centre, N.Y.: Freshet Press, Inc., 1971 reprint (original published 1921).
Outstanding book with a good overview of the history of tackle.

Skues, G. E. M. *The Way of a Trout with a Fly*. London: A. & C. Black, 1921.
Fine handling of fly patterns and some other tackle notions, very advanced for the day.

Foote, John Taintor, *The Wedding Gift*. New York: D. Appleton & Company, 1924.
The greatest tackle fantasy of all time—do read it if possible.

Hewitt, Edward R., *Hewitt's Handbook of Fly Fishing*. New York: The Marchebank Press, 1933.
Hewitt trumpets his own elegant tackle with other interesting items thrown in.

Bergman, Ray, *Trout*. New York: Alfred A. Knopf, Inc., 1938.
  Lots of tackle, dated but still fascinating.

Knight, John Alden, *Modern Fly Casting*. New York: Putnam, 1942.
  Discussion of the then-developing theory and practice of modern fly tackle.

Herter, George Leonard, *The Professional Split Bamboo Rod Building Manual*. Waseca, Minn.: Herter's Company, 1949.
  A mixed bag of pleasant surprises from the Herter's gang that enables you to do what its title suggests.

Kreider, Claude, *The Bamboo Rod and How to Build It*. New York: Macmillan & Company, 1951.
  A semisequel to Holden's book, more of five-strip and general coverage.

McClane, A. J., *The American Angler*. New York: Henry Holt & Company, 1954.
  Early treatment of glass and other things by a true expert.

Gingrich, Arnold, *The Well-Tempered Angler*. New York: Alfred A. Knopf, Inc., 1965.
  Musings, mostly on ultralight tackle, by a true enthusiast of the sport—but don't take it too seriously!

Melner, Sam, and Kessler, Herman, *Great Fishing Tackle Catalogs*. New York: Crown Pubs., Inc., 1972.
  Pretty compilation of old-time pictures with prose by Sparse Grey Hackle.

Index

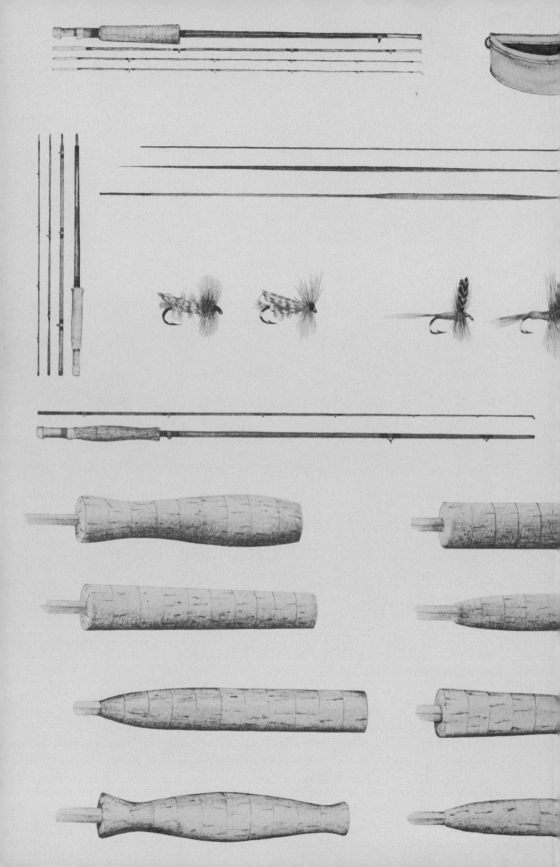